ENGLISH
LANGUAGE

Life

&
CULTURE

Anne Fraenkel
Richard Haill
Seamus O'Riordan

TEACH YOURSELF BOOKS

For UK order queries: please contact Bookpoint Ltd, 130 Milton Park, Abingdon, Oxon OX14 4SB. Telephone: (44) 01235 827720. Fax: (44) 01235 400454. Lines are open from 9.00–18.00, Monday to Saturday, with a 24-hour message answering service. Email address: orders@bookpoint.co.uk

For USA order queries: please contact McGraw-Hill Customer Services, P.O. Box 545, Blacklick, OH 43004-0545, USA. Telephone: 1-800-722-4726. Fax: 1-614-755-5645.

For Canada order queries: please contact McGraw-Hill Ryerson Ltd., 300 Water St, Whitby, Ontario L1N 9B6, Canada. Telephone: 905 430 5000. Fax: 905 430 5020.

Long-renowned as the authoritative source for self-guided learning – with more than 30 million copies sold worldwide – the *Teach Yourself* series includes over 200 titles in the fields of languages, crafts, hobbies, sports, and other leisure activities.

British Library Cataloguing in Publication Data
A catalogue entry for this title is available from The British Library.

Library of Congress Catalog Card Number: on file

First published in UK 2002 by Hodder Headline Plc, 338 Euston Road, London NW1 3BH.

First published in US 2002 by Contemporary Books, A Division of The McGraw-Hill Companies, 1 Prudential Plaza, 130 East Randolph Street, Chicago, Illinois 60601 U.S.A.

The 'Teach Yourself' name and logo are registered trade marks of Hodder & Stoughton Ltd.

Copyright © 2002 Anne Fraenkel, Richard Haill & Seamus O'Riordan

Typeset by Transet Limited, Coventry, England.
Printed in Great Britain by Cox & Wyman Ltd, Reading, Berkshire.

| Impression number | 10 | 9 | 8 | 7 | 6 | 5 | 4 | 3 | 2 | 1 |
| Year | 2006 | 2005 | 2004 | 2003 | 2002 | | | | | |

CONTENTS

Acknowledgements

The authors and publisher are grateful to the following for
permission to reproduce copyright material in this book:

The Guardian: one extract (p. 113) from 'Do the British get enough
bank holidays?', Claire Phipps, 31 March 1999.

Punch Ltd.: one cartoon by Pav (p. 49).

INTRODUCTION

This book is designed to give you as full a basic overview as possible of the main aspects of England: the country, its language, its people, their way of life and culture and what makes them tick. It is important to bear in mind that the book is about *England* and its language and culture, not the whole of the United Kingdom, although many aspects, especially social ones, will be common to all or most of the UK.

Many people use the terms 'England/English' and 'Britain/British' interchangeably. In fact, however, 'England' is the country bordered by Wales to the west and Scotland to the north. 'Britain' should really only be used to mean 'Great Britain', which comprises England, Wales and Scotland, or for the 'United Kingdom', itself short for the 'United Kingdom of Great Britain and Northern Ireland'. Many Scots and Welsh will understandably get very upset if they are referred to as 'English'!

You will find it a useful foundation if you are studying for examinations which require a knowledge of the background of England and its civilization, or if you are learning the language in, for example, an evening class and want to know more about the country and how it works. If your job involves travel and business relations it will provide valuable and practical information about the ways and customs of the people you are working with. Or if you simply have an interest in England for whatever reason, it will broaden your knowledge about the country and its inhabitants.

The book is divided into three sections:

■ **The making of England**
   Chapters One and Two deal with the forces – historical, geographical, geological, demographical and linguistic – that have brought about the formation of the country we know as

England and the language we know as English. Chapter Two also takes a look at the international role of English.

- **Creative England**

  Chapters Three to Seven deal with the wealth of creative aspects of English culture from the beginnings to the present day. These chapters take a look at the main areas or works of literature, art and architecture, music, traditions and festivals, science and technology, fashion and food and drink, together with the people who have created and are still creating them.

- **Living in England now**

  Chapters Eight to Eleven deal with aspects of contemporary English society and the practicalities of living in present-day England: the way the political structure of the country is organized, education, the environment, the workplace and how people spend their leisure time. The final chapter looks at the country's political, economic and social relations with the wider world, and takes a glance at the future.

Taking it further

Each chapter ends with a section entitled 'Taking it further', where you will find useful addresses, websites, suggested places to visit and things to see and do in order to develop your interest further and increase your knowledge.

The language

If you wish to put your knowledge into practice, we have provided in each chapter a list of useful words and phrases to enable you to talk or write about the subject in question.

We have been careful in researching and checking facts, but please be aware that sources sometimes offer differing information. Of course a book of this length cannot contain everything you may need to know on every aspect of England. That is why we have provided so many pointers to where you can find further information about any aspect that you may wish to pursue in more depth. We trust that you will enjoy this introductory book, and that it will provide leads to further profitable reading, listening and visiting.

Phil Turk
Series Editor

1 | THE MAKING OF ENGLAND

The land

England is the largest of the three countries that make up the island of Great Britain, with an area of about 130,000 sq km, compared with 78,000 sq km for Scotland and 21,000 sq km for Wales. Its borders are partly the result of geography, and partly the legacy of ancient politics. To the east and south, and part of the west, England is bounded by the sea. To the north, its border today is only a short distance north of the limit settled by the Romans nearly two thousand years ago. Around AD 130, during the reign of the Emperor Hadrian, the Roman conquerors of Britain built a stone wall from the west coast to the east to separate their colony from Scotland. Although they later occupied some of lowland Scotland, it was only for a short time. The wall, known as Hadrian's Wall, can still be seen. To the west, England's border with Wales follows close to the line of an earth bank and ditch built by Offa, King of Mercia (now the English Midlands) towards the end of the eighth century to mark the boundary of his kingdom, and to defend it from attacks by the Welsh. Again, Offa's Dyke, as it is called, is still visible today.

Lowlands, uplands, rivers and lakes

The English landscape is determined mainly by the different types of rock underlying it. In the south, chalk has produced the gently rolling hills of the Downs, while hard granite is the basis for the mountains of the north and the high moorlands of Exmoor and Dartmoor in the south-west. Most of England is fairly low – less than 100 m above sea level – apart from parts of the north and the south-west, and even its highest areas are less than 1000 m above sea level. Its landscape has also been shaped by natural processes of wind, water, ice and frost, as well as by the effects of human settlement and agriculture. For the greater part of the last 2 million years, England was covered in a thick layer of ice, and the movement of great glaciers has left deep U-shaped valleys in some of its upland areas such as the Cumbrian Mountains. Many of these valleys have filled with water to form lakes, which is why the area is more commonly known as the Lake District. This is the only part of England where there are lakes of any significant size. It is an area of great beauty which has long attracted artists and poets (notably Wordsworth and Coleridge) as well as tourists.

The highest mountain in England is Scafell Pike (978 m) in the Cumbrian Mountains, where there are also several other high peaks, including Helvellyn (950 m), Skiddaw (930 m) and Bow Fell (902 m). In the whole of the rest of England there are only five other peaks which can be called mountains (that is, which are over 600 m above sea level – the usual definition of a mountain in England). Three of these are in the Pennines, a long range running north to south like a backbone through northern England; another is in the Cheviot Hills in Northumberland, close to the border with Scotland; and the fifth is on Dartmoor (High Willhays, 621 m).

England's best-known river is, of course, the Thames which flows through London. It is also the longest, at 346 km. (The River Severn is longer in total, but its source is in the mountains of Wales, and the part that runs through England is shorter than the Thames). Other great English rivers include the Trent, the Great Ouse, the Tyne, and the Nene which all flow into the North Sea, and the Mersey, which flows into the Irish Sea at Liverpool.

The coast

England's coastline is very varied. There are spectacular chalk cliffs like those of Beachy Head or Dover, and rocky cliffs like many round the coast of Devon and Cornwall in the south-west. But there are also areas of flat land: freshwater wetlands, saltmarshes, and mudflats, such as the coast of East Anglia, as well as beaches of sand or pebbles. Like the rest of the landscape, the coastline has changed over time, and is still changing: waves, tides and currents have eroded some areas, and extended others by

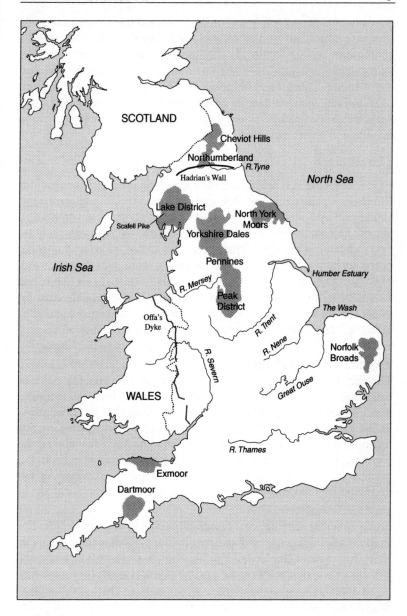

England

depositing sand and silt. Parts of the coast just north of the Humber estuary in the north-east of England are disappearing at the rate of nearly 3 m a year, while in the south, Romney Marsh and the Dungeness peninsula have been growing since Roman times, and the Roman shore-line is now several miles inland. Human intervention, too, has had an effect, with the building of ports and harbours, and coastal defences such as sea-walls to try to prevent erosion and protect the land.

The climate

England has a fairly mild and temperate climate, though the weather is also very variable from day to day, which probably explains why so many people think it rains all the time! In reality, the rainfall is moderate, with all the central and eastern parts of England having less than 750 mm a year, and only the upland areas of the north-west and south-west receiving more than that (between 750 mm and 1500 mm). The prevailing winds blow from the Atlantic Ocean to the south-west, but England is also affected by masses of air blowing from other sources – cold air from the Arctic to the north and from the northern continent to the east, and warm air from the south. This is one of the reasons why England's weather is so changeable.

The southern part of England is generally warmer than the north in the summer, and has more hours of sunshine, while in winter the west is warmer than the east. But the temperature is rarely extreme in any part of the country, and it does not often rise above 32°C, or fall below –10°C. This is mainly because of the influence of the surrounding sea, which takes longer than the land to heat up in the summer, and longer to cool down in the winter. The waters of the Gulf Stream, a current which flows from the tropics, also help to keep the land mass warmer.

Some unusual weather has occurred in recent years, as it has in many other countries, and this may be a sign that the climate is changing. For example, the summer of 1996 was the driest since records of weather began to be kept in the eighteenth century, while April 1998 was the wettest since 1818 (source: Office of National Statistics).

National Parks

There are seven National Parks in England: Northumberland, the Lake District, the Yorkshire Dales, the North York Moors, and the Peak District in the north of England, and Exmoor and Dartmoor in the south-west. Together with the Norfolk Broads in the east (a special protected area), they cover almost 10,000 sq km, 8 per cent of the whole area of England. Most of them are privately owned, and are called 'national' parks in recognition of their importance to the nation. The purpose of designating national parks is to conserve their natural beauty and wildlife, and to allow the public to enjoy them. There are also about thirty-five places which are designated as Areas of Outstanding Natural Beauty so that they can be protected, though this does not necessarily mean they are made more accessible to the public.

The English regions

Different parts of England look very different; the landscapes are varied, there are different patterns of agriculture, and the local materials used for building homes also affect the appearance of each area. In addition there are considerable variations in density of population, in the ways people live and work, and in economic prosperity.

London and the south-east

The countryside is gently hilly, with two ranges of low chalk hills stretching from west to east across the region. The North Downs meet the sea with the famous white cliffs of Dover, while the South Downs also spectacularly meet the sea at Beachy Head. Between them is the Weald, once a large forest and still wooded in many places. Villages are close together, and there are many towns of varying size. The coast is densely populated, with a string of ports and seaside resorts so close together it is often difficult to see where one ends and the next begins. Many English people used to take their holidays in the seaside resorts of the south coast, but as the cost of flying and package holidays abroad have got cheaper, these resorts have declined, but are a popular location for retirement homes.

Regions and cities of England

London covers a huge area, some 1600 sq km, and is the largest city in Europe. Through the middle of London, from west to east, flows the great River Thames, and some of the city's most famous buildings are found on, or close to, its banks: the Houses of Parliament, the South Bank, St Paul's Cathedral, and the Tower of London, to name just a few. Many visitors to London notice how green it is. There are many parks and open spaces, and relatively few very tall buildings. In the centre of London, the area known as the West End contains a large number of theatres, museums and art galleries, while to the east, the City of London (built on the site of the Roman city of Londinium) is one of the world's great financial centres. Further east, the old Docklands area, once derelict, has become a showcase for some of the most innovative modern British architecture. It is dominated by Canary Wharf, and is served by two new transport routes: the Docklands Light Railway, and an extension to the Jubilee Line (part of the underground railway system, also known as the 'Tube').

If you look at a map of England, you will notice how roads radiate out across the country from London like the spokes of a wheel.

The south and south-west

In the centre of the southern part of England lies Salisbury Plain, a relatively flat area with very few trees, and famous for its prehistoric stone circles at Stonehenge and Avebury. This great chalk plain marks the beginning of the chalk hills of south-east England – the North and South Downs and the Chilterns – while to the west, the shapes of huge horses and men have been cut out of many of the chalk hillsides. It is an area of both sheep and arable farming. Further south on the coast are the busy ports of Southampton and Portsmouth, from where ferries sail to France and Spain.

The south-west peninsula of England, often known as the West Country, has a very different character from the rest of southern England. The coast is rocky and the climate is particularly mild; frost is rare, and palm trees grow in some places. It is one of the most popular parts of England for holidaymakers.

East Anglia

The area south of the Wash, north of London, and east of the A1, the old road to the north originally built by the Romans, is mostly rural. There are many towns, but only Norwich, Ely and Cambridge count as cities, and they are fairly small. The land is relatively flat, with gently rolling hills, which provides excellent farmland, good for both sheep and crops. In fact East Anglia is the most productive agricultural region of England. The area called the Norfolk Broads is full of lakes ('broads') and rivers, and many people go there for boating holidays in the summer months.

The Midlands

The southern boundary of the Midlands lies on a line drawn from the River Severn to the Wash; to the west is the border with Wales, to the east is the North Sea. In the north the Midlands extend as far as Merseyside, Greater Manchester and Yorkshire. During the nineteenth century this region was the industrial heart of England, and though many of the old iron and steel industries have declined, it is still an important industrial centre. Birmingham is England's second largest city, with over a million inhabitants. To the north of Birmingham, the area round Stoke-on-Trent is known as the Potteries, which has long been famous for the fine china produced there. Wedgwood is probably the best-known china, but the area is also the home of Minton and Spode.

The Midlands also contain some pretty, rural areas, as well as the wild and beautiful landscape of the Peak District, an area of bare limestone hills popular with walkers.

The north

From the River Mersey in the west and the River Humber in the east to the border with Scotland in the north, the north of England contains some of the wildest and most beautiful scenery in the country. In the centre, the Pennines range runs north to south. In the north-west is the Lake District containing Scafell Pike and the other Cumbrian peaks mentioned above.

Either side of the Pennines are the large industrial cities of Liverpool, Manchester, Leeds, and Hull, but further north the population is very sparse.

History

The history of England is, of course, very closely linked to the history of the other countries of the United Kingdom – Scotland, Wales and Northern Ireland – but in this account we shall focus mainly on England, only referring to the other countries when necessary.

Early history

The Roman province of Britannia included only what is now England and Wales; to the north, very close to the present border between England and Scotland, the Romans built a massive stone wall (known as Hadrian's Wall) which you can still see today. The Romans occupied Britain for nearly four hundred years, and their main lasting influence was probably the introduction of Christianity. During the fourth century the province was attacked by Germanic tribes from northern Europe – the Angles, the Saxons and the Jutes. In fact the name 'England' comes from 'the Angles'. When the Romans left in AD 409, the invaders eventually settled down with the earlier inhabitants, and a number of small kingdoms were established in what is now England.

Over the next few centuries, first Kent, then Mercia, then Wessex became the dominant kingdom, but in the ninth century Danish invaders – the Vikings – took control of the northern and eastern parts of England, leaving the south and west under the control of the Anglo-Saxon kingdom of Wessex. King Alfred the Great of Wessex strengthened his border with the Danelaw (the part of England ruled by the Danes). Most people remember him as the king who burnt the cakes. One day, he came to a woman's house; she didn't recognize him as the king, and asked him to watch her cakes which were baking in the oven. But Alfred was thinking about his military plans and forgot the cakes. When the woman came back, the cakes were burnt, and she was very angry. Alfred apologized, and went away without telling her that he was the king.

Eventually, in the tenth century, Wessex and the Danelaw came under the control of one king, who was now known as the King of England. A few of the early English kings were Danish, but most were Anglo-Saxon. In 1066, England was attacked by William, Duke of Normandy, who fought with King Harold at the Battle of Hastings. Harold was killed, and on Christmas Day, William the Conqueror was crowned king of England in Westminster Abbey. 1066 is probably one of the best-known dates in English history because it was the last time an invasion of England was successful.

The Middle Ages (twelfth to fifteenth centuries)

Although he was king, William and his Norman soldiers did not feel entirely safe in England because many of the Anglo-Saxons remained hostile. William took land away from the English lords, and gave it to his soldiers who built strong stone castles where they could live and control the local population. The Tower of London is the greatest of these castles. Some twenty years after he became king, William ordered his officials to compile a detailed record of all the property, and who owned it, in every town and village of the country. This record was known as the Domesday Book. It showed that by this time only two Anglo-Saxon lords still kept their estates; the lands of all the others had been transferred to French lords. The French-speaking barons and lords ruled over the English-speaking peasants, and so the English class system began. For the next four hundred years, the Kings of England were all of French origin, and it was not until 1327 that England had a king who could speak English. Henry IV, who came to the throne in 1399, was the first native English speaker to become king.

Although kings were very powerful at this time, two important developments laid the foundations for today's political and legal system. In 1215 the barons forced King John to agree that the power of the king could be limited by law, and throughout the medieval period judges appointed by the king travelled around the country hearing cases. The jury system also developed at this time; a group of ordinary people (all men in those days!) decided whether the person accused was guilty or innocent. The barons and the senior clergy – bishops and archbishops – began to meet regularly to advise (or put pressure on) the King. This assembly was referred to as a 'parliament', and in the thirteenth century it started to include representatives from every city and rural area. These representatives eventually met separately from the lords, and so the structure of our modern parliament was born. The two chambers are still called the House of Commons and the House of Lords.

In the middle of the fourteenth century a terrible disease, known as the Black Death, killed nearly half the population of England. As a result there was a shortage of labour, and at the same time more land was available for the peasants who survived.

The Middle Ages were a time of frequent wars. England was at war with France for almost a hundred years, as English kings tried to protect lands they owned in France, or to claim more land. For thirty years in the middle of the fifteenth century, two rival families fought for the English crown in the Wars of the Roses, so called because the symbol of one family, descended from the Duke of York, was a white rose, while the symbol of the other, descended from the Duke of Lancaster, was a red rose. The wars finally ended when Henry Tudor, son of a Welsh knight, came to the throne and united the two families.

Tudor England (1485–1603)

The double Tudor rose combined the white rose of York and the red rose of Lancaster, and can be seen in the decoration of many buildings and in paintings of this period.

Tudor rose

England was changing from a small and relatively unimportant nation on the northern edge of Europe into a much more powerful one. Merchants trading in English woollen cloth and other goods were becoming more prosperous, helped by the growing numbers of English ships that sailed around Europe and beyond. Henry Tudor (Henry VII) spent a great deal of money on the navy, including his flagship, the *Mary Rose*. As it sailed out of Portsmouth harbour for the first time, it sank. A few years ago, it was found and raised, and you can now see it in the museum in Portsmouth.

This was a time of exploration and discovery, as ships sailed further and further to the east and west, to what was then called the 'New World' and which we know as America. Virginia, one of the states, was named after Elizabeth I, who was the granddaughter of Henry VII and known as the Virgin Queen because she never married (though in reality she had many lovers!).

The Tudor age was also a time of religious disputes. In many parts of northern Europe there was dissatisfaction with the corruption of the clergy and the power of Rome, and at the same time a feeling that the ideas of the Christian religion should be more accessible to ordinary people. Until now, the Bible and all church services were in Latin, but translations into local languages began to appear. In England, both the Bible and the Book of Common Prayer were published in English for the first time. However, the pressure for religious change in England was also political. Henry VIII desperately wanted a son, but his wife had only produced a daughter. He asked the Pope to allow him to divorce his wife, but the Pope refused. So Henry persuaded parliament to pass the Act of Supremacy, recognizing the English monarch as the head of the Church in England instead of the Pope. Henry then got his divorce and went on to marry five more times. He also used his new power as head of the Church to close the monasteries and to take control of church lands, making himself very rich in the process.

Civil War and the Restoration of the monarchy (seventeenth century)

England as a whole got richer during the sixteenth and seventeenth centuries, but those who earned wages got poorer. Prices were rising much faster than wages, and in the villages much of the common land where poor people could keep their animals was being fenced off by local landowners for sheep or to grow corn. Many poor people could no longer make a living in the countryside, and moved to the towns and cities to look for work. But the growth of urban populations simply increased the demand for food from the country, and the richer farmers bought up more and more land to satisfy this demand, at the same time causing more poor people to move away.

Elizabeth I had no children so when she died, her cousin James Stuart, who was already King of Scotland, became King of England too. From then on the two countries had the same monarch, though they continued to have two separate Parliaments for another hundred years. The Tudor kings and queens had provided strong government for England, but James and his son Charles found it difficult to keep the nobles and other powerful men on their side. The nobles constantly argued with parliament about taxes, and MPs (Members of Parliament) complained about the power of the King's advisers. Eventually this led to the Civil War between Charles I and his supporters, the Royalists, and those MPs who opposed him. Charles was captured, tried and executed, and Oliver Cromwell, an MP who had led the opposition army, was made 'Protector' of the new republic. Cromwell closed the theatres and banned dancing. After Cromwell's death, Charles' son (Charles II) was invited to become king, but with more limited power. In particular, the king could no longer impose taxes without the agreement of parliament.

Religious arguments continued all through the seventeenth century. Catholics were treated with hostility. By the end of the century a new law stated that the monarch had to be a Protestant and could only marry a Protestant (this is still the case today). There were also arguments amongst the Protestants. The Puritans (like Cromwell) believed that the Church of England was too much like the Roman Catholic church, and thought that church services should be much simpler. Puritans were persecuted too, until James II persuaded MPs to allow them to have their own religious services. However, they were not allowed to become MPs or go to university.

The industrial revolution and urban growth (eighteenth century)

The growing number of overseas colonies, established originally by English trading companies, made the country more and more wealthy. English ships traded all over the world, exporting coal, cloth, guns and other manufactured products and importing goods like cotton, sugar, tobacco and tea. They were also involved in the profitable slave trade between Africa and the Caribbean.

Woollen cloth had always been an important export, spun and woven by country people in their own homes. But when new machinery was invented for spinning and weaving, cloth manufacture moved to factories. Other industries were changing too. Henry Cort found a way of using coal instead of charcoal to make cast iron, James Watt discovered how to make a steam engine turn a wheel and power machines in factories, and George Stephenson developed the first railway locomotive, to name just a few of the many new inventions of the age. The coal-mining industry also expanded rapidly, as coal was now used to power industrial production such as sugar refining, glassmaking and brickmaking and not just for domestic cooking and heating.

New methods of farming meant that England could produce enough food to feed itself and export some as well, so food was cheap. Though the great majority of people were still agricultural workers, increasing numbers of people were needed for industrial production, especially in the Midlands and the north of the country. Towns and cities were growing rapidly, and so was the population of the country as a whole. Between 1500 and 1800 the population of England went up from just over 2 million to well over 6 million.

Good transport was increasingly important, and since the roads were just muddy tracks, canals were dug all over the country to provide a faster and more reliable system of transport.

London was now the largest and richest city in Europe, with a population of around a million. It was an important financial centre; merchants could borrow money from its banks to buy goods, or take out insurance in case one of their ships sunk, and people could also buy and sell shares in trading companies through stockbrokers.

Political and social reform (eighteenth and nineteenth centuries)

When Queen Anne died childless in 1701, the English parliament asked George of Hanover, a Protestant descendant of James I, to become king in order to prevent the Catholic son of James II coming to the throne. George I did not speak English, only German and French, and so he left the administration of the country to a committee made up of members of the majority party in parliament, and chaired by their leader. This was in effect a prime minister with a cabinet, the form that the executive takes today. Sir Robert Walpole, who held this position for over twenty years, was not only the first prime minister but also the first to live at 10 Downing Street, which has been the home of British prime ministers ever since.

Parliamentary reform was long overdue. The system had hardly changed since 1430, and was clearly unfair. Only one person in a hundred could vote; some seats belonged to lords who simply nominated an MP; and some seats had hardly any voters, while the new industrial towns like Birmingham and Manchester had no MPs at all. Yet the House of Lords and many MPs were strongly opposed to any change. It was only with difficulty that a law was finally passed in 1832 extending the vote to the majority of middle-class men. Another important political reform later in the century was that ballots were to be secret.

The nineteenth century was also a time of great social reform. The slave trade was abolished, laws were passed to regulate the employment of women and children in factories, primary schools were established wherever there were no church schools, and men could no longer be excluded from universities or politics because of their religious beliefs. But the Poor Law forced poor people out of their homes and into the dreadful conditions of workhouses, described so vividly by Charles Dickens in *Oliver Twist,* and was the cause of much discontent amongst the working classes.

Queen Victoria ruled from 1837–1901, and the word 'Victorian' came to be used to describe the beliefs and values of middle-class people of this time, with an emphasis on the importance of family, religion, hard work, self-control and respectability.

The twentieth century

Political developments in the early part of the twentieth century include a decline in the power of the House of Lords, and a corresponding increase in the power of the House of Commons. Women known as 'Suffragettes' demanded that they should be allowed to vote in parliamentary elections, but it was not until 1918 that women over 30 were given the vote, and another eleven years before this was extended to all women and men over 21. Trade unions had been established in the later part of the nineteenth century; they continued to grow, and the Labour Party which they founded replaced the Liberal Party as the alternative to the Conservatives. For the first time, the working classes had a real political voice.

Social developments have included free primary and secondary education for all children, pay for workers who are sick, state pensions for the retired, and a free health service for all. These developments and other recent events in England are dealt with in more detail in the rest of this book.

Time chart

409	Roman government of the British Isles ended
1066	William the Conqueror (the Duke of Normandy) defeated Harold and became King of England
1086	The Domesday Book
1215	King John signed the Magna Carta
1337	Start of the 100 Years' War between England and France
1348–9	Black Death – nearly half of the English population died
1381	Peasants' Revolt
1455–87	Wars of the Roses
1477	William Caxton printed the first book in England
1534–40	The Reformation
1542	Act of Union united England and Wales
1558–63	Queen Elizabeth I
1603	The kingdoms of Scotland and England were united when James VI of Scotland became James I of England
1642–51	The English Civil War between the king and parliament
1649	Charles I was executed and England became a republic
1653–58	Oliver Cromwell ruled as Protector
1660	Restoration of the monarchy under Charles II
1665	The Great Plague

1666	The Fire of London
1687	Publication of Isaac Newton's *Principia*
1707	Act of Union united the English and Scottish Parliaments
1805	Battle of Trafalgar
1815	Battle of Waterloo
1825	The world's first passenger railway opened between Stockton and Darlington
1832	Reform Act
1837–1901	Reign of Queen Victoria
1859	Charles Darwin published *On the Origin of Species*
1907	The first Rolls-Royce motor car was built
1914–18	The First World War
1918	Women over 30 given the vote
1939–45	The Second World War
1948	Free medical care for everyone was introduced – the National Health Service
1952	Queen Elizabeth II came to the throne
1965	Natural gas was discovered in the North Sea
1969	Oil was discovered in the North Sea
1973	The UK joined the Common Market, now called the European Union
1979–90	Margaret Thatcher was the UK's first woman prime minister
1994	The Channel Tunnel joining England and France opened for trains
1997	The Labour Party won the general election for the first time since 1979
1999	A Scottish Parliament and a national assembly for Wales were set up, taking back some of the powers they had lost more than 200 years before
2002	Queen Elizabeth II's Golden Jubilee

GLOSSARY

arable suitable for growing crops

ballot system of secret voting using pieces of paper

baron a member of the lowest rank of the nobility

border the line that separates two countries

colony a country that is controlled by another country

common belonging to everyone, not to an individual

derelict no longer used, and so falling into ruins

ditch a narrow channel dug into the ground

estuary the mouth of a river; the part where it flows into the sea

glacier a large mass of ice that moves slowly down a mountain valley

granite a type of very hard grey rock

limestone a type of rock containing calcium

monarch a king or queen; a ruler who is not elected

peak the pointed top of a mountain

peasant a person who works on a small piece of land they own

range a connected line of mountains or hills

silt soil carried by flowing water and then dropped, for example, at the mouth of a river

supremacy the state of having the highest power

temperate having tempeartures that are neither very high nor very low

Taking it further

Suggested reading

Halliday, F E, *England: A concise history*, Thames and Hudson, 1995

Hibbert, Christopher, *The Story of England*, Phaidon Press, 1992

Kimpton, Laurence, *Britain in Focus*, Hodder and Stoughton, 1990

O'Driscoll, James, *Britain*, Oxford University Press, 1995

Websites

For information about travel and tourism in England, try **http://www.travelengland.org.uk**

A website that has useful information about English history is **http://www.britainexpress.com/history**

2 THE ENGLISH LANGUAGE

English is not just the language of England; it is the first language of most of the inhabitants of the British Isles (which includes the Republic of Ireland as well as the United Kingdom) and it is also spoken by many millions of people in other countries around the world. According to David Crystal, author of *The Cambridge Encyclopedia of the English Language*, around 350 million people speak English as their first language. He also claims that perhaps as many as 300 million also speak English as a second or official language, with several hundred million more speaking English as a foreign language. English is now used very widely as the language of international communication, and perhaps the majority of conversations in English today are between people who are not native speakers of the language. How did this happen? In this chapter we shall be looking at how English developed in England, and at some of the reasons why it has become so widely spoken internationally.

There are many different types of English. The variety an individual speaker uses depends on where they live, or their social class, or education, or even on the particular situation they are in. As we shall see later in this chapter, most people speak more than one variety of English.

The origins of English

When Germanic invaders arrived in England in the fifth century, they spoke a language that was called after one of their tribes, the Angles. The language, known as *englisc*, provided the basic grammatical structures of modern English, as well as most of our everyday words. Even now, more than 80 per cent of the thousand most common words survive from Old English. But if you heard this language today you would not understand it at all because of the enormous changes that have taken place in the past fifteen hundred years.

Pronunciation

Pronunciation changes have mainly affected the vowel sounds. Beginning in the twelfth century and continuing until the eighteenth century, all the long vowel sounds changed. So in Chaucer's time, *mine* would have had the same vowel as modern *mean*, while *mouse* would have sounded like *moose*. This is known as the Great Vowel Shift. Most consonants have not changed, though a few new ones (like the sound of the 's' in measure) have been added. In most accents in England today, we do not pronounce all the letter 'r's that occur in the spelling, so *father* and *farther* sound exactly the same. Originally all the 'r's were pronounced, as they still are in south-west England and in some parts of the north of the country (and, of course, as they are in Scotland, Ireland, and most of the United States and Canada). We do not really know why people started to drop their 'r's; it was probably just a fashion that caught on. There are many other consonant sounds that used to be pronounced but which are not pronounced in modern English. Just think of the silent letters in words like *know, write, talk, lamb* and *caught!*

Grammar

One of the main grammatical changes is that English has lost most of its word-endings. For example, nouns used to have different endings according to their case, but the only ones that survive today are the plural ending *-(e)s* and the possessive *'s*. The meanings that used to be expressed through other endings are now conveyed by prepositions such as *to, for* or *from*.

An interesting example of grammatical change is the way we use the present continuous tense (also called the present progressive). In Shakespeare's time it was not very common; and so we find a character in *Hamlet* asking: *'What do you read?'* where today we would expect *'What are you reading?'* to refer to something that is happening at the time of speaking. Now, the present continuous is also used to talk about the future: *I'm meeting him tomorrow*; and the 'going to' form has become increasingly common: *I'm going to meet him tomorrow.*

Vocabulary

The greatest changes have been in the vocabulary of English, which has grown enormously, mostly by borrowing words from other languages. Nobody knows exactly how many words there are in English, because it is so difficult to count them. There are many slang and other colloquial words some of which are used for a short time and then disappear, while others may be used for many years before they appear in dictionaries. There are also a lot of very specialized words belonging to electronics, or industrial processes, or an obscure branch of medicine, for example. There are probably at least half a million English words, and perhaps as many as a million. Less than 30 per cent are of Germanic origin. To understand how this has come about, we need to look at the different political and social events that have influenced the development of English. As you will see, in many ways the history of English reflects the history of England.

Throughout its history, English has borrowed words very freely from the languages it has come into contact with. The Vikings gave us words like *both, give* and *same,* and the pronouns *they, them* and *their.* As we saw in Chapter One, the Norman rulers spoke French, while the rest of the people spoke a kind of English that included more and more French words. Perhaps it is not surprising that most of these came from topics that particularly concerned the French nobility: politics *(parliament, government)*, the law *(judge, prison)*, religion *(prayer, saint)*, defence and the army *(castle, enemy)*, and luxury goods *(satin, diamond)*. Most of the words for cooked meat *(pork, beef, mutton)* come from French, while we still use the Old English words for the animals themselves *(pig, cow, sheep)*, because it was the English serfs who looked after them.

The influence of printing

By the end of the Middle Ages, both French and Latin were in decline, as the descendants of the Norman kings now felt they were

English rather than French, and as the power of the Church became less. William Caxton's printing press gave many more people access to books, and the number of people who could read and write grew. Within one hundred and fifty years, about twenty thousand different books were published. Caxton had to decide what kind of English to use in his books, because there were still many different dialects. He chose the dialect of the East Midlands, an area that included London, because it was the dialect spoken by many merchants, because people in both the north and the south of England could understand it, and because it was already used for most official documents. Spelling was also fixed at around this time, though it was very much influenced by French spelling. For example, the word *house* was pronounced with a long 'oo' sound (as in *food*), which was spelt *ou* in French.

Many of the books published were translations of foreign authors, and there was enormous interest in the writings of classical Greece and Rome. Translation was often difficult because English did not have equivalent words for the ideas to be translated, and so huge numbers of words were borrowed. The majority came from Latin, either directly or through French, while many others came from Greek, French, and Italian. Examples include (from Latin) *dexterity, notorious, peninsula, area, capsule*; (from Greek) *anonymous, catastrophe, tragedy, skeleton*; (from French) *passport, detail, entrance*; (from Italian – especially words related to music) *sonata, concerto, soprano, violin*. In the sixteenth and seventeenth centuries, English merchants and explorers were travelling around the world, and consequently words also came into the language from many other sources. For example, *algebra, almanac, saffron, orange, sugar,* and *zero* came from Arabic, through other languages. Many words came from the Americas through Spanish, including *chocolate, tobacco, maize* and *hurricane*. From Turkish we got *coffee* and *kiosk*, from Persian *bazaar* and *caravan*, while *yacht, smuggle, sketch* and *landscape* were all borrowed from Dutch.

English continued to borrow words from other languages throughout the eighteenth and nineteenth centuries, and well into the twentieth century. As the British Empire developed and flourished, and trade and travel became easier English borrowed from more and more languages, bringing us words like *mammoth* and *apparatchik* from Russian; *pyjamas* from Urdu; *loot, jungle* and *shampoo* from Hindi; *tycoon* and *satsuma* from Japanese; *robot* from Czech; and *curry* from Tamil.

Varieties of English

In the past, people in different parts of England spoke dialects of English that differed from each other quite a lot in vocabulary, pronunciation and grammar, and people from different areas could not necessarily understand each other easily. Today the main differences are in pronunciation, and most people speak with an accent that shows the region of England they come from. We have already mentioned that people in the south-west and in some parts of the north pronounce all the letter 'r's in the spelling, while people in the rest of the country only pronounce 'r's that are followed by a vowel sound. All across the north of England and much of the Midlands words like *butter* and *come* have the same vowel sound as *put* and *good*, and words like *path* and *grass* have the same vowel as *cat*. Differences like these help to identify where an English speaker comes from.

The way we speak or write also varies depending on where we are (eg at home, in the pub, at work), who we are talking or writing to (eg a small child, a friend, a prospective employer), the topic under discussion (eg last night's football match, a friend's serious illness), and the type of interaction (eg a job interview, a business letter, buying something). So individual English speakers also have a range of styles to choose from.

Standard English

Standard English is the form of the language generally used in print and in the speech of most educated people. It is usually accepted that this term refers to grammar and vocabulary, but not everyone agrees that it can refer to pronunciation as well. The issue of standard English has always aroused strong feelings, and to this day the debate is confused by the different meanings of the word 'standard'. As an adjective, it has the meaning 'usual', (as in 'standard procedure'), while as a noun it can mean either 'a level of quality' or 'a moral value'. The idea of standard English is influenced by all these meanings, and it is clear that different people use the term differently.

We have already seen that in the fourteenth century the introduction of printing, and the ability to produce large numbers of identical copies of books, made standard grammar, vocabulary, spelling and punctuation necessary.

In 1702, John Kersey produced a twenty-eight-thousand-word dictionary of English which was essentially a guide to correct spelling. Several dictionaries of hard words were published around this time to help those readers who had not had a classical education. In 1755, Samuel Johnson's dictionary appeared. He set out to list all the words in English with their correct spelling, their origin and their meaning, and he used quotations from literature to illustrate their use. Most of the spellings in Johnson's dictionary are the same today, nearly two hundred and fifty years later.

After the Restoration of the monarchy in 1660, there was a growing interest in trying to 'fix' the language, by establishing norms and rules to prevent the language from changing in ways considered undesirable. In 1664, the Royal Society set up a committee for improving the English language. Several people proposed there should be an academy for the English language like those of Italy and France. The academy was never established, but the strong belief in correctness and in the need to regulate the language, formed during this period, has formed part of the debate about standard English ever since.

Religion was an important factor in spreading the standard dialect. The first translation of the Bible into English appeared in 1526, the Book of Common Prayer was published in 1549, and the Authorized (or King James) Version of the Bible in 1611. The last two of these had a particularly powerful influence in establishing standard English. Wider acceptance of the standard forms in later centuries was also helped by the spread of literacy and education.

Received pronunciation

Guides to pronunciation began to appear in the eighteenth century. Generally, their model was the pronunciation used by middle-class Londoners. Although the accent known as received (accepted) pronunciation (RP) is often described as having been promoted by the public school system during the nineteenth century, there is very little evidence to support this view. It may not have been until the very end of the nineteenth or early twentieth century that the upper-class accent was standardized. Today we can recognize several forms of RP: 'conservative' RP, spoken by older people like the Queen; 'general' RP spoken by younger people (and sometimes known as 'BBC English'); and 'modified' RP, a form of RP with some regional features.

According to David Crystal, as few as 3 per cent of the population speak 'pure' RP, while other educated people speak 'modified' RP. It is the most comprehensively described accent of English, it is the pronunciation given in dictionaries, and the variety taught to foreigners, but the relatively small number of speakers makes it questionable how far it can really be regarded as the standard pronunciation. It seems, if anything, to be losing its prestige, which may explain the increasing use of 'Estuary English' (see below) amongst the younger upper classes.

English around the world

In the early seventeenth century, Protestant Christians from England began to settle on the east coast of America. They wanted to find a place where they could practise their religion without persecution. Many others soon followed, some for religious reasons, otherwise simply hoping for a more prosperous life. Over the next two or three hundred years, as British trade expanded around the world, English-speakers also settled in Australia and New Zealand. Trade, and the growing British Empire, established English as an important means of communication in many parts of Africa, Asia, and the islands of the Caribbean. This is why English today is the first language of most of the inhabitants of the United States, Canada, Australia and New Zealand, and is the second or official language of countries like India, Singapore, Kenya and Nigeria. It is also spoken both as a first and as a second language in multiracial South Africa. Though the similarities between all these varieties of English are greater than the differences, each has its own characteristics. Distinctive accents are the most noticeable distinguishing features, but there are also some differences in vocabulary and occasionally slight differences of grammar as well.

When the Soviet Union collapsed in 1989, it left only one superpower in the world – the United States. The rapid spread of English as the main language for international communication is mainly because so many people recognize the power and influence of the United States. But other factors have also been important. Hollywood has helped, of course, as well as the American media, especially television. American films and TV programmes are seen all over the world.

Three circles of English

The American linguist Braj Kachru has divided the world's users of English into three concentric circles: in the Inner Circle are those countries where English is spoken as a mother tongue, in the Outer Circle are the countries where English has a role as an official language, and finally in the Expanding Circle we find the countries where English is learnt as an international language (see opposite).

How English is changing

We have already seen that English has changed enormously over the centuries. But English, like all languages, is never finally fixed, and so it continues to change all the time. Some people feel that these changes are bad, and mean that the language cannot express ideas as precisely as it used to, or that people are 'sloppy' or careless in the way they use it. But most people accept that changes are natural and inevitable, as our ideas and way of life also change. Our grandparents did not need words like *Internet, software, disco, credit card, skateboard* or even *teabag,* because none of these things existed when they were young! English vocabulary is growing fast, especially in the areas of science and technology, but also in politics, work, and the media, for example.

The Expanding Circle
English as a foreign or international language,
e.g. Japan, France, Germany, Russia, China, Egypt, Brazil

The Outer Circle
English as a second or official language,
e.g. India, Singapore, Nigeria, Ghana,
Kenya, the Philippines

The Inner Circle
English as a mother tongue,
e.g. UK, USA, Australia,
Canada, New Zealand

The Circles of English

New words

Today, borrowing from other languages is less frequent than in the past, and most new words are created out of English itself. The most common way is to combine two words to create a new compound word, and there are huge numbers of these (e.g. nouns: *laptop, frogman, hatchback, software, blockbuster, double-decker, boy band*; verbs: *short-change, double-park*; adjectives: *child-proof, over-optimistic*). As you can see, they are sometimes written as a single word, sometimes with a hyphen, and sometimes as two separate words. Since dictionaries rarely agree, this is not worth worrying about!

New words can be created using affixes (these include **prefixes** that are added at the beginning, and **suffixes** that are placed at the end). The suffix -*ish* meaning 'approximately' has given us *fortyish* and *youngish*, while the prefix *e-* (meaning 'electronic') is currently producing large numbers of new words, such as *email, ecommerce, e-business* (sometimes a hyphen is used, sometimes not – the spelling of this new prefix has not been fixed yet).

There are a number of other ways of making new words, such as shortening an existing word (*sitcom* from *situational comedy*), blending two words together (*smog* from *smoke* + *fog*; *docudrama* from *documentary* + *drama*), or using the name of a person for something associated with them. These are called 'eponyms', and one of the best-known examples is the word *sandwich*, named after the Earl of Sandwich who (it is said) asked his servants to bring him a meal he could eat while he continued to play cards! A more recent one is *hoover*, which is the word most people use for a vacuum cleaner.

Pronunciation change

One kind of pronunciation change which is noticeable today is the way many long words are stressed. There seems to be a trend towards putting the main stress on the third syllable from the end. Compare how the following words were pronounced a hundred years ago with the way they are usually pronounced today:

1902	2002
ab′domen	*′abdomen*
an′chovy	*′anchovy*
′hospitable	*ho′spitable*
in′explicable	*inex′plicable*
se′cretive	*′secretive*

Estuary English

In the last twenty years or so, people have noticed a tendency, especially among young people, to use an accent which is a mixture of RP and the London accent, and which has been described as 'Estuary English', because it was first noticed in the area around the estuary of the River Thames. However, it is now heard much more widely across the southern and eastern parts of England. Radio and television presenters, and celebrities of all kinds use this accent, probably because RP is now so unfashionable – no-one wants to be accused of 'talking posh'!

Grammatical change

Grammatical change is slower and less frequent, but we can still see signs that English continues to lose inflections, as it has for the past thousand years. Most grammar books will tell you that adjectives with one syllable or with two syllables ending in -*y* form the comparative and superlative by adding -*er* and -*est*, as in *taller* and *happiest.* But it is increasingly common to find adjectives of this kind using *more* and *most,* as longer adjectives do (for example, *more beautiful* or *most enjoyable*). Recent examples include *more keen* and *most lovely.* And the distinction between *will* and *shall*, still explained in many grammar books, in practice has almost disappeared except amongst a few elderly speakers. *Will* is now the universal form, with *shall* found only in the expressions *Shall I ..?* (offering to do something) or *Shall we ...?* (making a suggestion).

The future

How might English change in the future? Of course, it is difficult to say exactly what the language will be like in a hundred years' time, but we can imagine what may happen if the kinds of changes that we can see at the moment continue. The vocabulary will almost certainly continue to expand, and American English will go on influencing most other varieties of English, including the English spoken in England. This is likely for two main reasons: more than half the native speakers of English in the world are American, and the United States is politically and economically the most powerful nation on earth. In England we may see a change in the pronunciation of educated people, continuing the trend for Estuary English. Political devolution in Wales and Scotland is already bringing calls for devolution of power to the English regions.

People are beginning to value and celebrate the differences in culture and language that are characteristic of their region. As RP loses its prestige, and regional accents gain a more equal status, people may use a modified RP with some elements of a regional pronunciation. It is possible that there will no longer be an English accent that identifies only the social status of the speaker.

Around the world, there are two ways in which English may develop. All the different varieties could become more and more similar, as people travel more and have to communicate with other people speaking different kinds of English. Or we may find that people are keen to preserve the characteristics that make their variety of English different from others, and so there may be greater and greater differences between the Englishes spoken around the world. Perhaps in the end these Englishes will develop into different languages (just as, hundreds of years ago, Latin developed into Italian, French, Spanish and the other Romance languages). If that does happen, we may also find that people use a new World Standard English as a means of international communication. Time will tell!

Playing with words

Q. How do you get down from an elephant?
A. You don't. You get down from a swan.

This joke exploits the fact that the word *down* has two different meanings (it is an adverb of direction, and also a noun meaning 'the soft feathers of a duck or swan', used, for example, to make pillows). There are many jokes like this in English, partly because there are so many **homonyms** – words that have the same form but different meanings. Also, the English love to play with words. Here is another joke based on homonyms:

Two parrots are sitting on a perch, and one turns to the other and asks, "Can you smell fish?"

Look up the word *perch* in your dictionary to find its two different meanings!

We call this kind of play on words a **pun**. Here are some more (to make them easier to understand, the homonym is written in bold type):

*What makes a tree noisy? – Its **bark**.*

> *Have you heard the story about the woodpecker? –*
> *Yes, it's **boring**.*
>
> We also make puns with **homophones** – words that sound the same, but have different spellings and different meanings:
>
> *When does a baker follow his trade? – Whenever he needs (kneads) the dough.*
>
> *What's black and white and red (read) all over? – A newspaper.*
>
> *When is a car not a car? – When it turns into a garage.*
>
> Other types of word-play include palindromes, words or expressions that read the same backwards as they do forwards (*Was it Eliot's toilet I saw?*). Finally, try these tongue twisters:
>
> *She sells seashells on the seashore.*
>
> *Red leather, yellow leather, red leather, yellow leather, ...*
>
> That is quite enough of this nonsense!

Learning English

If you are able to read this book without too much difficulty, you have already reached a very good level of proficiency in English. But if you want to go on making progress, the rest of this section has some suggestions for areas to work on.

Reading for pleasure

One of the best ways of improving your English is to read as much as you can. What do you enjoy reading in your own language? Try to find similar kinds of books or magazines in English. Or use the internet to find English-language websites on subjects that interest you. Read as much as you can, and do not worry too much about words that are new to you, so long as you get the general idea. It is not always necessary to use your dictionary; you will probably find you understand a new word after meeting it several times in context.

Synonyms

Because English has borrowed so many words from other languages, it now has many pairs of words with similar meanings, usually with different origins. For example, *fast* (which comes from Old English) and *rapid* (which comes from Latin). But it is extremely rare for two words to have exactly the same meaning; one usually has a more negative or positive meaning, or perhaps one is more formal than the other. If we say someone is *slim*, we are admiring them, but if we call them *skinny*, we think they are too thin and ought to eat more. *Tell* and *relate* mean almost the same, but *relate* is more formal, and is less likely to be used in spoken English.

There are many pairs of synonyms that include a phrasal verb:

go on – continue
make out – pretend
take in – deceive
throw out – reject
find out – discover
put off – postpone

Many learners find the single word synonyms (*continue, pretend, deceive, reject*, etc) easier to learn. Unfortunately it is the phrasal verbs that are the ordinary everyday forms, while the others are more often found in written English.

So when you find a word that seems to mean the same as another one you already know, try to find out how the two words are different. Here are some questions to ask:

Can I use this word in speaking, or is it too formal?
Does it have a positive or negative meaning?
Is one of these words used much more frequently than the other?

Collocations

Language students often learn lists of new words, but it is also important to learn words that go together. For example, when you learn a word like *effort* it is useful to know that the verb that goes with it is *make* and not *do*. Also, it is important to learn that the adjective *interested* is often followed by the preposition *in*. Words that go together are called 'collocations'; make sure you include them in your vocabulary notebook.

Learners often complain that native speakers talk too fast. One of the reasons native speakers of any language, not just English, can speak quickly is that a lot of what they say is ready-made. Short expressions, phrases and even whole sentences are used again and again, and can be produced automatically by a native speaker whenever they want to. So while most language students learn individual words, native speakers learn whole 'chunks'. Here are some examples:

By the way ...
I see what you mean.
What are you having? (Offering to buy someone a drink)
If you want my advice, you'll ...

Listen for expressions like these and put them in your notebook too.

Pronunciation and spelling

Many learners despair of ever understanding the relationship between English spelling and pronunciation. The problem comes mainly from the fact that spelling was fixed hundreds of years ago, and reflects English pronunciation as it was at the time. It is also because English has forty-four different speech sounds, while there are only twenty-six letters in the alphabet. Even by the sixteenth century people were beginning to complain that spelling was not close enough to pronunciation. John Hart wrote a book in 1569 called *An Orthographie*, in which he proposed a completely new spelling system based on pronunciation. Over the centuries others have wanted to reform English spelling, including the playwright George Bernard Shaw, who illustrated the problem by claiming that the word *fish* could just as easily be spelled *ghoti* – if you take the *gh* from *laugh,* the *o* from *women*, and the *ti* from *nation*!

But Shaw was wrong, because *gh* can only be pronounced *f* when it comes at the end of a word (as in *enough* and *cough*); and *ti* is only pronounced *sh* when it is followed by a vowel (as in *cautious* or *Martian*). So there are some rules, and you can find books that help you to learn them (see the suggestions at the end of this chapter).

Perhaps the best thing you can do to help yourself is to learn to read the phonetic alphabet, so that when you look up a word in your dictionary you can also learn how to pronounce it.

Study the phonetic symbols in the box below, and then see if you can read the following jokes:

Vowels		**Diphthongs**	
/iː/	f<u>ee</u>t, b<u>ea</u>n	/eɪ/	r<u>ai</u>n, d<u>ay</u>, th<u>ey</u>, m<u>a</u>ke
/ɪ/	f<u>i</u>t	/eʊ/	s<u>o</u>, s<u>ow</u>, s<u>ew</u>, th<u>ough</u>, ph<u>o</u>ne
/e/	b<u>e</u>d, s<u>ai</u>d	/aɪ/	f<u>i</u>ne, h<u>igh</u>, b<u>uy</u>
/æ/	b<u>a</u>d	/aʊ/	h<u>ow</u>, ab<u>ou</u>t
/ɑː/	h<u>a</u>rd, f<u>a</u>ther, c<u>al</u>m	/ɔɪ/	b<u>oy</u>, b<u>oi</u>l
/ɒ/	g<u>o</u>t	/ɪə/	h<u>ere</u>, h<u>ear</u>
/ɔː/	c<u>ou</u>rt, c<u>au</u>ght, s<u>aw</u>	/eə/	th<u>ere</u>, h<u>air</u>, b<u>ear</u>, b<u>are</u>
/ʊ/	p<u>u</u>t, f<u>oo</u>t	/ʊə/	p<u>ure</u>
/uː/	c<u>oo</u>l, t<u>u</u>ne		
/ʌ/	s<u>u</u>n, s<u>o</u>n		
/ɜː/	b<u>ir</u>d, h<u>ur</u>t, h<u>ear</u>d, w<u>or</u>k		
/ə/	<u>a</u>bove, f<u>or</u>get, wat<u>er</u>		

Consonants			
/p/	<u>p</u>ot, ca<u>p</u>tain	/s/	<u>s</u>ell, pla<u>c</u>e
/b/	<u>b</u>ell, o<u>b</u>vious	/z/	<u>z</u>ero, plea<u>s</u>e, card<u>s</u>
/t/	<u>t</u>own, looke<u>d</u>	/ʃ/	<u>sh</u>oe, ma<u>ch</u>ine, educa<u>ti</u>on
/d/	<u>d</u>oor, a<u>dd</u>ress	/ʒ/	mea<u>s</u>ure, televi<u>si</u>on
/k/	<u>c</u>ook, lu<u>ck</u>y, a<u>c</u>tor	/h/	<u>h</u>ill, be<u>h</u>ind
/g/	<u>g</u>ood, u<u>g</u>ly	/m/	<u>m</u>an, roo<u>m</u>
/tʃ/	<u>ch</u>eap, ma<u>tch</u>	/n/	<u>n</u>ine, se<u>n</u>t
/dʒ/	<u>j</u>udge, a<u>ge</u>	/ŋ/	so<u>ng</u>, thi<u>nk</u>
/f/	<u>f</u>ifty, <u>ph</u>one	/l/	<u>l</u>et, te<u>ll</u>
/v/	<u>v</u>ery, lea<u>v</u>e	/r/	<u>r</u>ose, so<u>rr</u>y
/θ/	<u>th</u>in, ten<u>th</u>	/j/	<u>y</u>ou, <u>y</u>es
/ð/	<u>th</u>is, mo<u>th</u>er	/w/	<u>w</u>ait, <u>wh</u>en

Two phonetic jokes

Q. /wɒt də ju kɔːl ə bɪldɪŋ wɪð lɒts əv stɔːrɪz/

A. /ə laɪbrɪ/

Q. /waɪ ɪz ɪt deɪndʒərəs tə pleɪ kɑːdz ɪn ðə dʒʌŋgəl/

A. /bɪkɒz ðər ə səʊ menɪ tʃiːtəz/

(Clues: storeys/stories; cheetahs/cheaters)

Other languages spoken in England

There are no longer any other indigenous languages spoken as a first language in England apart from English. The last native speaker of Cornish (a Celtic language related to Welsh and once spoken in the south-west of England) is often said to have been a woman called Dolly Pentreath who died in 1777, but it seems likely that a few speakers remained until the end of the eighteenth century. Cornish gradually died out as English became the main language of commerce, and also because it was thought of negatively as the language of poor and uneducated people. However, since the early 1900s there has been a movement to revive Cornish, and there are now a small number of people who speak it as a second language.

It is very difficult to estimate how many people in England have different first languages, but a recent survey found that over 300 languages are spoken in London schools. Apart from English, the top ten mother tongues are: Bengali, Punjabi, Gujerati, Hindi/Urdu, Turkish, Arabic, Yoruba, Somali, Cantonese and Greek. Of course, London is much more cosmopolitan than the rest of England, but all the big cities are now ethnically very mixed and have large populations from Asia, the Middle East and Africa who speak English at school or at work, but who very often speak another language at home. You can find out more about the people of England and how they came here in Chapter Eleven.

GLOSSARY

accent the way someone pronounces words

affix a sound or letter, or a group of sounds or letters, added to the beginning or end of a word to change its meaning or how it is used

case the form of a noun or pronoun that shows its relationship to other words

chunk a large piece of something; a fixed expression

collocation the way in which some words regularly go together

colloquial used in ordinary everyday conversation; not formal

cosmopolitan containing people from many different countries

dialect the form of a language used in one area

homonym a word that sounds the same, and is spelt the same, as another word, but has a different meaning

homophone a word that sounds the same as another, but is spelt differently and has a different meaning

indigenous originating in a particular place

inflection a word-ending added to change the grammatical function of the word

literacy ability to read and write

norm a standard that is typical or average

phrasal verb a group of words that acts like a single-word verb, and consists of a verb and an adverb and/or a preposition

prestige the state of being respected or admired

pun humorous play on a word with two meanings

serf a farm worker in the Middle Ages

slang very informal language, not always polite, and not always in use for long

synonym a word that means the same as another word

Taking it further

Suggested reading

Culpeper, Jonathan, *History of English*, Routledge, 1997

Knowles, Gerry, *A Cultural History of the English Language*, Arnold, 1997

Bryson, Bill, *Mother Tongue*, Penguin Books, 1991

Crystal, David, *The Cambridge Encyclopedia of the English Language*, Cambridge University Press, 1995 (or a much shorter and easier read by the same author: Crystal, David, *The English Language*, Penguin Books, 1998)

Studying English in England

Studying at a language school or college in England is an excellent way to improve your English, and to experience life in England at the same time. The British Council regularly inspects organizations in England and the rest of the United Kingdom that offer courses in English as a foreign language. If they meet high standards of quality they are 'accredited by the British Council'. So if you want to study here, make sure that the school you enrol with is an accredited one.

Websites

Michael Quinion's 'World Wide Words', is a website that focuses on British English and covers a wide range of interesting topics. You can find it at: **http://www.worldwidewords.org/**

'Dave's ESL Café' is an American site, run by teacher Dave Sperling, with lots of exercises and practice activities for learners of English; and it is also a place to find penfriends from all over the world to correspond with in English. You can find it at: **http://www.eslcafe.com**

The British Council provides a list of English language schools in Britain that it has inspected and approved at the following website: **http://www.britishcouncil.org/english/courses**

A useful website about Estuary English is kept up-to-date by Professor John Wells of the Department of Phonetics and Linguistics at University College London: **http://www.phon.ucl.ac.uk/home/estuary/home.html**

3 | ENGLISH LITERATURE

English literature can be compared to a large orchard full of lovely fruit: here in the centre you have many fine old trees still producing the best, over there are a few which look tired and are not giving much now, while round the edges of the orchard you have some small but interesting varieties whose fruit some people love but others have no taste for. It would be hard to do the richness of this orchard full justice in a book of a thousand pages, let alone 20 or so. Therefore, this chapter will aim to give you just a taste of the best that has been produced, while also showing you some of those less well-known varieties that may be worth trying.

First, we shall take a look at the two best-known geniuses of English literature, Shakespeare and Dickens. Then we shall select some examples from poetry, drama and the novel, not forgetting other areas in which English literature has made a special mark, such as the detective novel, comic writing and books for children.

This chapter is only concerned with the work of English writers, and therefore the following – though several lived in England for most of their lives – are not included:

- **Irish** writers: Swift, Goldsmith, W B Yeats, Shaw, O'Casey, Synge, Wilde, Joyce, Beckett, Heaney.
- **Scots** writers: Smollett, Walter Scott, Burns, Stevenson, Barrie, Conan Doyle, Buchan, Irvine Welsh.
- **Welsh** writers: Dylan Thomas, Jean Rhys, R S Thomas.

Shakespeare

Of course the tree standing above all others in the landscape is **William Shakespeare** (1564–1616). There are libraries full of books on Shakespeare, and his works have been analyzed from every angle, yet his plays remain as popular – and are still as relevant – as ever. Not only are they performed in almost every country in the world, but they have also given inspiration to other great international artists:

Shakespeare in music, dance and film

Art form	Composer/ Director	Works
Opera	Verdi	*Macbeth, Otello, Falstaff*
	Wagner	*Das Liebesverbot* (based on *Measure for Measure*)
Ballet	Prokoviev	*Romeo and Juliet*
Classical works	Liszt	*Hamlet*
	Schumann	*Julius Caesar*
	Sibelius	*The Tempest*
	Mendelssohn	*A Midsummer Night's Dream*
	Tchaikovsky	*Romeo and Juliet*
Musicals	Bernstein/ Sondheim	*West Side Story*
	Cole Porter	*Kiss Me Kate*
Film music	William Walton	*Henry V*
Films	Orson Welles	*Othello, Macbeth*
	Olivier	*Henry V, Hamlet, Richard III*
	Polanski	*Macbeth*
	Kurosawa	*Throne of Blood (Macbeth), Ran (King Lear)*
	Zeffirelli	*The Taming of the Shrew, Romeo and Juliet*
	Branagh	*Much Ado about Nothing, Hamlet*

Shakespeare's work has also been 'modernized' in hundreds of different productions, often in surprising but very effective ways, eg *Othello* in a colonial setting, *Macbeth* as a big business power struggle, *A Midsummer Night's Dream* with magic tricks, *Richard III* as a fascist politician, and so on. This shows that Shakespeare's work – his characters, his poetry, his ideas – still has a universal meaning which each artist can use to express his or her own vision for our time.

In England today, Shakespeare has his 'own' theatre company (The Royal Shakespeare Company, see Chapter Six) and his 'own' theatres, in Stratford, his native town, and in London on the South Bank, where the Globe Theatre – a replica of the one where Shakespeare and his group of actors performed in the early seventeenth century – was built in the 1990s. So, there is little doubt that Shakespeare still has a major role in the nation's cultural life.

The Globe Theatre

Dickens

The only other major English literary figure whose work can be said to come close to equalling Shakespeare in both prestige and continuing popularity is **Charles Dickens** (1812–1870). Each had a genius for bringing characters and ideas to life: while Shakespeare could show in poetry or prose the thoughts of kings and princes just as well as those of porters or grave-diggers, Dickens' special ability lay mainly in plot and character, in describing common – often poor or criminal – people and the greatest city in the world in the nineteenth century, London, where most of his novels are set.

Dickens' earlier work, including *The Pickwick Papers* and *David Copperfield*, is loved for its sense of fun and the number of humorous characters it contains, while his later 'darker' novels, (eg *Bleak House, Dombey and Son, Little Dorrit*) tend to have more serious social themes, and have achieved greater praise from critics. Through his novels Dickens hoped to bring to the reading public's attention some of the terrible social injustices which existed at that time, such as the poverty and cruelty in London slums, the poor quality of prisons and schools, the inefficiency of government. His novels are long but very readable because Dickens has a gift for both telling a good story and bringing to memorable life people, places and scenes. Some of his characters – Pickwick, Oliver Twist, Fagin, Micawber, Gradgrind, Miss Havisham – have become part of the national memory.

Poetry

Someone once said that it is surprising that a nation whose people so lacked a poetic spirit could still have produced so much great poetry! A good starting-point in this beautiful part of the orchard is **Geoffrey Chaucer** (1340?–1400), as he was the first major poet in the English language, and is usually the first to be read by students taking courses in the history of English literature. Chaucer went on a pilgrimage (a journey to a special religious place) to Canterbury in 1388, and later wrote the masterpiece for which he is most famous, *The Canterbury Tales*, a collection of stories told (in verse) by pilgrims on their way to Canterbury.

The Elizabethan Age

English poetry of the Elizabethan Age (the reign of Queen Elizabeth I from 1533 to 1603) was particularly rich, with **Spenser**, **Sidney**, **Marlowe**, **Shakespeare**, **Marvell**, **Donne**, and **Jonson**, all writing then. The songs, odes and sonnets of the time dealt with the classical themes of love and its pains, honour and duty, the pleasures of country life. Many of these lovely poems still hold great appeal for modern readers.

Alexander Pope

Alexander Pope (1688–1744) was one of England's finest poets and critics. His masterpiece was *The Rape of the Lock*, a 'mock-heroic' poem which took an unimportant subject (the cutting off of a lock of the hair of a young woman) and treated it as if it was a matter of the greatest seriousness. The poem both satirizes the manners of his day and gives a wonderful picture of fashionable life then (the clothes, wigs and jewellery, the river trips, the card-games, the parties). Pope also wrote epigrams, essays in verse, translations from the Greek poets and witty attacks on fellow poets. His work is always a model of elegance and clarity.

The Romantic movement

Many fine poets emerged in England during the eighteenth century. **Thomas Gray** (1716–1771) and **William Blake** (1757–1827) were, in their different ways, precursors of the Romantic movement which swept across literary Europe at the end of this period. Gray was known above all for his *Elegy in a Country Churchyard*, which is still one of the most popular and most quoted poems in the English language. Blake was a poet, artist and visionary who lived and died in poverty. His lyrical poems often showed his fascination with the contrast between innocence and experience, and still seem fresh, original, full of joy and beautiful imagery. Blake wrote two poems which live on today in different forms: *The Tiger* (in every anthology of children's verse) and the idealistic poem, *Jerusalem*, which was put to music by the English composer Hubert Parry in 1915 and soon became a kind of second National Anthem, sung at conferences, demonstrations, sporting events and the Last Night of the Proms (see Chapter Six).

In 1798 **William Wordsworth** (1770–1850) and **Samuel Taylor Coleridge** (1772–1824) jointly produced a volume of poetry entitled *Lyrical Ballads*. This was perhaps the start of a movement called the Romantic Revival, which broadly includes other poets such as Walter Scott, Lord Byron, Southey, Shelley and Keats, though each was very different in temperament, politics and poetic style. At least Wordsworth, Coleridge and Southey had the Lake District in common. This lovely part of north-west England is where Wordsworth was born and from where he took the inspiration for much of his moral attitudes and his poetry. The three shared – like Rousseau in France and Goethe in Germany – a passion for solitude and communion with Nature, and a belief in the value of individual experience, both in childhood and adulthood.

Coleridge was also addicted to opium for much of his life. Nevertheless, he was a genius who produced two of the greatest, and most imaginative, poems in the English language, *The Ancient Mariner*, about an old sailor who relates the fantastic happenings he experienced on a sea voyage, and *Kubla Khan*, an unfinished poem of powerful, dream-like imagery which Coleridge is said to have written under the influence of opium.

Lord Byron (1788–1824) was like a pop star in his day: if gossip columns had existed then, he would regularly have appeared in them. His exciting life (his noble birth, dark good looks, his love affairs, his quarrels, travels and adventures, his death in Greece) has tended to take attention away from his poetry, which is a pity as most of it is a pleasure to read, being full of wit, passion and rich imagery. His long poem, *Don Juan,* is perhaps his greatest work: Byron gives his own version of the story and travels of Don Juan, but makes the poem a serious criticism of contemporary society, though rich with colour, humour, adventure and wonderful rhymes.

John Keats (1795–1821) was the youngest of the great romantic poets, but the first to die (of tuberculosis, in Rome). His reputation is remarkable, given that he began writing poetry only at the age of 21. All he left were some wonderful letters, and a fairly small number of odes and sonnets, which showed that he was the equal of his great fellow Romantic poets. You read Keats' verse for its rich imagery and his dedication to the idea of beauty.

Victorians

As we have seen, during the Romantic movement England was blessed with several poetic geniuses, and two more were soon to follow in this great tradition: **Alfred Tennyson** (1809–1892) and **Robert Browning** (1812–1889). On Wordsworth's death in 1850, Tennyson succeeded him as Poet Laureate (a poet officially chosen to write poems on special state occasions such as battles, royal weddings and funerals). Two of Tennyson's best-known were *Ode on the Death of the Duke of Wellington* and, most famously, *The*

Charge of the Light Brigade. But these crowd-pleasing lyrics did not represent Tennyson's best work; like Keats, he was expert at using classical legends (such as the story of King Arthur and the Knights of the Round Table) to create a mood of dreamy melancholy. This aspect, combined with his wonderful gift for imagery, sound and rhythm, was typical of his best poetry, such as *In Memoriam, The Lady of Shalott* and *The Idylls of the King*.

Browning was a different kind of poet: he was more concerned with contemporary moral and social questions, and his poetry was more obscure, a lot of it having as a background the Italian Renaissance (the period from the fourteenth to the sixteenth century when there was intense interest in art and literature). His best and most memorable poems are his short lyrics, such as *My Last Duchess* and *Meeting at Night*.

Thomas Hardy

Although his novels will be discussed later, mention must be made here too of **Thomas Hardy** (1840–1928), as he was a fine poet whose influence on twentieth-century writers was considerable. It was not until his fifties that, annoyed by the poor reception of his last novel, *Jude the Obscure*, Hardy turned to poetry. He wrote poems which tended to look back with sadness and regret – as well as some humour – on incidents from his youth and marriage. His best poems are short, simple lyrics describing moments or memories which illustrate his rather gloomy view of the passing nature of life and happiness.

A E Housman

Hardy's near contemporary, **A E Housman** (1859–1936), was similar in that he published poetry relatively late in life and had a rather pessimistic view of the world. He produced one of the most popular volumes of poetry ever published in England, *A Shropshire Lad,* in 1896. These poems are set in the countryside of Shropshire and, like Hardy's poetry, have as their main themes the brief nature of life and love. Housman's best poems have a mood of sad and haunting beauty, to which generations of English readers have warmly responded.

Twentieth-century greats

Housman's poems, which often dealt with the tragic, early deaths of young men, were strangely prophetic since the next great phase of English poetry came out of the sorrow and pity of The Great War (1914–1918) in which so many young men died. Much fine and lasting poetry was written then, some by men who survived (**Siegfried Sassoon**, **Robert Graves**, **Edmund Blunden**) and some by those who did not (**Rupert Brooke**, **Wilfred Owen**, **Edward Thomas**). The poems of this period show the terrible reality of life in the trenches, as well as the comradeship of the men living together in that hell.

England can perhaps lay claim to five other poets of the twentieth century who have a worldwide reputation among critics and readers:

Poet	Dates	Collections of poems	Themes
T S Eliot	1888–1965	*The Waste Land, Four Quartets, The Journey of the Magi*	Emptiness of modern civilization, religious beliefs
John Betjeman	1906–1984	*Collected Poems, Summoned by Bells*	Childhood, churches, railways, Victorian architecture
W H Auden	1907–1973	*Collected Shorter Poems, Collected Longer Poems, About the House*	Politics, the classical world, philosophy, religion
Philip Larkin	1922–1985	*The Less Deceived, The Whitsun Weddings, High Windows*	Drabness and disappointments of modern life
Ted Hughes	1930–1998	*The Hawk in the Rain, Crow, Tales from Ovid*	Animals and the natural world, myths

Drama

Apart from the giant Shakespeare, which playwrights still have the power to shock, delight or thrill us today? In this section some of England's other great dramatists and their works will be described.

Ben Jonson

Ben Jonson (1573–1637) was a friend and contemporary of Shakespeare; he wanted to show – as Dickens did in the nineteeenth century – the London of his day as it really was, with all its vivid life, cruelty and greed. His best plays are *Volpone, The Alchemist* and *Bartholemew Fair.* He was buried in Westminster Abbey, with the phrase written above his tomb, 'O rare Ben Jonson'.

Restoration comedy

When Charles II was restored to the throne in 1660, after several years of Oliver Cromwell's strict rule, the theatres were reopened, and plays became freer, lighter and less moral in tone. Three playwrights in particular are associated with this lively period of drama: **George Etherege** (1635–1691), **William Wycherley** (1640–1716), and **William Congreve** (1670–1729). Their plays have rather weak plots, but the characters are rich and varied, the satire of human vanity brilliant, the dialogue fast and witty, and the costumes delightful. Try, for example, Etherege's *The Man of Mode,* Wycherley's *The Country Wife*, or Congreve's *The Way of the World.*

Sheridan

Richard Brinsley Sheridan (1751–1816) is the only truly great name in English drama in the very thin period which stretched from the Restoration comedies to Noël Coward in the 1930s. Sheridan continued the Restoration tradition in the sense that his plays were social satires with plots which usually involved various complicated misunderstandings between young lovers until everything finished happily for all. His two best plays, *The Rivals* and *The School for Scandal,* are full of brilliant wit, memorable characters and cleverly constructed scenes.

1930s and 1940s

After Sheridan, the best plays put on in England in the next hundred or so years were by Irishmen or Europeans! Powerful works by Ibsen, Strindberg, and Chekhov, together with comedies or dramas by the Irish-born Oscar Wilde, J M Synge, O'Casey and George Bernard Shaw dominated the English stage, while the comic operas of Gilbert and Sullivan (see Chapter Five) proved immensely popular in the Victorian age. It is not until we come to the 1930s and the dramatic verse plays of **T S Eliot** (see page 45) and **Christopher Fry** (b. 1907) or the comedies of **Noël Coward** (1899–1973) that we again find English writers (or American-English in Eliot's case) in a prominent role. Eliot wrote several plays in verse, *Murder in the Cathedral* (about the killing of Archbishop Becket in Canterbury Cathedral in 1170) and *The Cocktail Party,* being the most popular. Fry's *The Lady's not for Burning*, set in the Middle Ages, is his most successful work.

Coward, whose music is discussed in Chapter Five, had huge success with his comedies whose wit reminded audiences of Oscar Wilde. The best of these plays, such as *Hay Fever, Private Lives* and *Blithe Spirit*, still have great appeal and are regularly revived.

John Osborne

With *Look Back in Anger*, produced in 1956, **John Osborne** (1929–1994), created a turning-point in the history of English theatre. The play, which shocked audiences at the time, centres on Jimmy Porter, a rebellious young man who attacks the values and attitudes of post-war Britain. Osborne (and his character) was called an 'Angry Young Man' – the first of a new generation of writers to question what they saw as the restrictions and class snobberies of contemporary Britain. The play also helped to displace the kind of safe and familiar 'drawing-room' comedies and polite dramas which had dominated the English stage for over a generation. *Look Back in Anger* also represented what became known as 'kitchen sink drama': this aimed to bring to the stage life as lived – and language as spoken – by those below the middle classes. Plays were soon followed by novels and films in showing this new realism. Osborne himself went on to write other powerful plays which contained criticism of English life or attitudes; the best of these were *The Entertainer, Luther* and *Inadmissible Evidence.*

Harold Pinter

A contemporary of Osborne, **Harold Pinter** (b. 1930), has achieved even greater fame and critical success as a playwright, so much so that the adjective 'pinteresque' has entered the language. The term refers to the sense one normally gets in a Pinter play: of characters not really communicating, humour arising from characters' use of English, silences, something unexplained and menacing in the air. He was clearly influenced in his early work by the 'absurdist' plays of the Irishman Beckett and the Frenchman Ionesco, but Pinter's plays are unique in style and content: as with all the best playwrights, his work is fascinating to read as well as to see and hear. Pinter once said that his plays were funny up to a point – and it was because of that 'point' that he wrote them. His major plays are *The Caretaker, The Birthday Party, The Homecoming* and *No Man's Land.*

Tom Stoppard

Tom Stoppard (b. 1937) first came to fame with his play *Rosencrantz and Guildenstern are Dead* in 1966. This had at its centre two minor characters from Shakespeare's *Hamlet* whom we see having philosophical but comic dialogues in between their brief appearances in the other play. This was a brilliant idea, typical of Stoppard's work. *Jumpers* combines moral philosophy and acrobatics, while *Travesties* features the (true) coincidence of the Irish novelist, James Joyce, the leader of the Russian revolution, Lenin, and one of the founders of the Dadaist movement, the Romanian Tristan Tzara, all living in Zurich in 1917. As may be guessed, Stoppard is an intellectual, but one who likes good jokes: his plays show his gift both for witty dialogue and for the discussion of moral and philosophical questions.

Alan Ayckbourn

Alan Ayckbourn (b. 1939) is the most productive of all contemporary English playwrights and the most successful. To date he has written over 50 plays, and has become a multi-millionaire from their popularity around the world; he once had five plays running at the same time in London. His plays are social comedies – though sometimes with an underlying tragic element – which generally deal with the behaviour and attitudes of the middle classes. There is farce and verbal humour in his plays, but he also shows how cruel and selfish people can be when their polite social masks are dropped. His best-known plays are *Absurd Person Singular,* the trilogy *The Norman Conquests,* and his recent successes at the National Theatre in London, *Home* and *Garden,* two plays which are designed to run in two separate but adjacent theatres at the same time, so that characters can move from one play to the other. Ayckbourn enjoys such theatrical challenges!

You can find recommendations for other plays and playwrights in the 'Taking it further' section at the end of the chapter.

[Reproduced with permission of *Punch Ltd.*]

The novel

Although there had been various forms of story-telling in poetry
and prose before the eighteenth century, it was not until then that
the novel became firmly established as a type of literature. Three
outstanding English writers led the way in developing the novel
into a truly popular art form.

Defoe, Fielding and Sterne

Daniel Defoe (1660–1731) was the first in England to achieve
success with a novel, *Robinson Crusoe*, in 1719. The story, based
on a real incident, describes how the shipwrecked Crusoe has to
live alone for several years on a desert island. Defoe wrote the story
as if it was the autobiography of Crusoe, and his readers were
totally convinced by it, so clever and realistic was the way each
detail of his life on the island was described. The novel and its
theme are as popular today as they were then.

Henry Fielding (1707–1754) was a journalist, a lawyer and a
playwright before he came to the novel, and he put all his
experience of life into creating memorable dialogue and dramatic
scenes. His great work (in both senses) is one of the finest English
novels, *Tom Jones*, written in 1749. The plot of the novel is very
carefully organized, and the action covers a wide area of life –
country houses, busy inns, road travel on horseback, sword-fights,
London street-life. Fielding had a great influence on the English
novel, and it is easy to see a link between his novels and those of
Dickens a century later. In 1963 John Osborne adapted the novel
for the cinema: the wonderful film, directed by Tony Richardson,
won several Oscars and helped to make many new Fielding
readers.

Laurence Sterne (1713–1768) could, like Fielding, equally well
be included in a section entitled 'The Comic Novel' for he too
wrote a richly funny novel, but one very different from Fielding's.
His master-work is *The Life and Opinions of Tristram Shandy*, a
complex novel which in many ways is more modern than most
modern novels! The reader has to wait until about a quarter of the
way through the book before the hero is even born, and the

narrative is full of constant jumps in time, unfinished sentences, blank or black pages, and other tricks. Yet despite all these oddities, *Tristram Shandy* had a serious purpose: Sterne wished to show – in a comic way – that a narrative novel which describes a period of characters' lives in an ordered, logical sequence must be false because experience is continuous, and so all kinds of past or simultaneous actions have an influence on the mind of a character living in the present.

The Gothic novel

The three novelists described above all helped – in their different styles – to establish the popularity of the novel with the reading public and enabled later writers to build on this strong base. One unusual development at the end of the eighteenth century was the rise of the 'novel of terror' or Gothic novel. Such work has had an influence right down to the ever-popular horror films of today, especially those made in the 1960s and 1970s by Hammer Studios in England: these usually featured either Count Dracula or Dr Frankenstein and his monster. The whole Gothic movement came out of an interest – as with the Romantic poets – in medieval imagery, for example, ruined castles, wild mountain scenery, knights, and beautiful young women needing to be rescued. Gothic fiction added to this some elements of horror, with much reference to the supernatural, torture, dead bodies, ghosts, hauntings and nightmares. The most successful Gothic novelist was **Mary Shelley** (1797–1851) – wife of the poet – who wrote *Frankenstein* in 1817. During a stay in Switzerland, Byron had suggested to Shelley and his wife that they each write a ghost story: Mary's was clearly the winner. The book she wrote was actually a serious investigation of the dangers of scientific experimentation (Frankenstein's creation of the monster), and may be called the first work of 'science fiction', a genre which became popular worldwide in the twentieth century.

Jane Austen

Far greater in skill and intelligence than the Gothic novels are those of **Jane Austen** (1775–1817). Only four of her novels were published during her lifetime: *Sense and Sensibility* (1811), *Pride* *and Prejudice* (1813), *Mansfield Park* (1814) and *Emma* (1816). Two other novels were published after her death, *Northanger Abbey* and *Persuasion* (both in 1818). Jane Austen's novels all deal with the 'landed gentry', that is upper middle-class people who live in big houses in the country. On the surface, the basic plot is romantic: one or more young women are looking for suitable husbands. On another level the novels are a record of the attitudes and manners of a section of English society, and reveal – through the characters and the way they behave – the ideals Jane Austen thought most important: self-knowledge, intelligence, tolerance, and goodness of heart. Jane Austen may have written about a small eighteenth-century world, but she shows her understanding of central human experiences: love, pride, jealousy, snobbery, the restrictions and tensions of family life, the development of the human heart. Jane Austen's novels are still immensely popular today, as one can see from the films and TV serials regularly made from them.

Thackeray

W M Thackeray (1811–1863) wrote five novels, but it is his first, *Vanity Fair,* which is considered his greatest: it was published (in monthly parts, as many novels were at that time) in 1847 and 1848. It is a long, wide-ranging novel which describes the contrasting lives and adventures of two girls, Becky Sharp and Amanda Sedley: while Becky is 'sharp', clever, ambitious and rather dishonest, Amanda is quiet, virtuous and honest. It is no surprise that the readers were far more interested in Becky! She is indeed a wonderfully rich and fascinating creation. Thackeray described the book as a 'novel without a hero', and this reflects his approach to the society he describes and satirizes: there are no real heroes, the world he depicts is cruel, hypocritical, snobbish – in fact, the 'vanity fair' of the title.

The Brontës

The story of the three Brontë sisters, **Charlotte** (1816–1855), **Emily** (1818–1848) and **Anne** (1820–1849) is one of the most extraordinary in English literature. That these young women, living in an isolated part of Yorkshire with their difficult father and brother, with no encouragement from any source, each came to write a famous novel, is a true triumph of will-power and imagination. After many refusals, Charlotte was eventually able to get *Jane Eyre* published in 1847, the same year in which her sister Emily's only novel, *Wuthering Heights*, and Anne's *Agnes Grey*, also appeared. Tragedy followed soon after, with the deaths of Emily's brother and both sisters within the next eighteen months. Emily went on to publish three other novels, and finally married in 1854, a year before her death.

Jane Eyre was immediately successful, and remains as popular as ever today. Though its dialogue is rather unbelievable and the plot melodramatic, the power and passion of the story are what one remembers. *Wuthering Heights*, though far less popular at the time, is generally considered now to be the greater achievement, both for the complex way in which the story of Catherine and Heathcliff is told (using different characters as narrators) and for Emily Brontë's vivid imagination. The novel's portrayal of these characters against the background of the wild Yorkshire landscape has an intensity which most readers find unforgettable.

George Eliot

In the mid-nineteenth century women began to write and publish their work more than ever before. **George Eliot** (1819–1880), was a contemporary of the Brontës, and had an equally unusual – though less tragic – life. In the rather strict and hypocritical Victorian age many found George Eliot's unconventional personal life shocking. Her real name was Mary Anne Evans; she fell in love with a married man, George Lewes, and, when she was 35, decided to live with him, which she did until his death in 1878. Two years later, and six months before her own death, she married.

Lewes encouraged her to write fiction, and she soon found success under her new name. Her key works are *Adam Bede, The Mill on the Floss, Silas Marner* and, above all, *Middlemarch*, which is her masterpiece. This, like many nineteenth-century novels, is very long, but the brilliant way in which George Eliot blends the social, working and interior lives of her characters makes the novel a richly satisfying experience. It is perhaps her skilful characterization, in particular of her heroine, Dorothea Brooke (sensitive, determined, generous – in a sense, a mirror of George Eliot herself), that one admires most of all.

Thomas Hardy

The last great novelist of this rich period of English fiction is **Thomas Hardy**, whose poetry was mentioned earlier in the chapter. He wrote novels until he was 56, when he turned to poetry. Like George Eliot, Hardy depicted a rural world: his was the county of Dorset in the south-west of England (he used the old English name, Wessex), and it is here that all his novels are set. One of his earliest, *Under the Greenwood Tree,* is his lightest and most charming picture of country life. His later novels show a deeper and darker side. Hardy believed in determinism, that is, he thought that our lives, like nature, follow certain pre-determined paths, and that every event has an earlier cause. His novels reflect this view, particularly in the way that his characters may struggle against fate. His five best novels – *Far from the Madding Crowd, The Return of the Native, The Mayor of Casterbridge, Tess of the D'Urbevilles* and *Jude the Obscure* – have elements of tragedy, but are also memorable for the way they portray the realities of country life: the poverty and hardship, the harshness and beauty of the landscape, the kindness and cruelty of individuals. We appreciate Hardy's gift for telling a gripping story but also for showing that ordinary people can in their own way be tragic or heroic figures too.

Joseph Conrad

Conrad (1857–1924) was born in Poland and joined the merchant navy as a young man. He stayed in the navy for over twenty years, collecting many of the experiences which would later find their way into his fiction. He felt he would not be widely read if he wrote in Polish, and, though he spoke French equally well, he decided to write his first novel in English. (His style was always careful, and rather formal.) His early novels and stories, such as *The Nigger of the Narcissus* and *Lord Jim,* used as their background the Eastern islands and oceans he knew so well. Perhaps his most famous work is *Heart of Darkness*, written in 1902. This short novel, only ninety or so pages in length, was a striking depiction of the colonial exploitation so common in that period, and was later the basis for the successful American film, *Apocalypse Now*, made in 1979. It is clear that Conrad's exciting adventure stories and romantic characters appeal to readers and film-makers alike. His later novels, such as *Nostromo, The Secret Agent* and *Under Western Eyes*, show that he was interested too in the political and moral dilemmas of his characters when faced with extreme situations.

Colonial themes

During the Victorian age, Britain hugely expanded her empire, at one stage administering almost a third of the world's land and population. This experience began to be reflected – as we have seen with Conrad – in the country's literature. Several writers of this era, and of our own time, have produced work which shows their reactions to this phase of English history:

Novelist	Dates	Countries written about	Best-known works
Rudyard Kipling	1865–1936	Indian sub-continent	*Barrack-Room Ballads* (poems), *Kim, Plain Tales from the Hills* (fiction)
E M Forster	1879–1970	India	*A Passage to India*
George Orwell	1903–1950	Burma	*Burmese Days*
Graham Greene	1904–1991	Africa, the West Indies	*The Heart of the Matter, A Burnt-out Case, The Comedians*
Doris Lessing	b. 1919	Zimbabwe	*The Grass is Singing, The Golden Notebook*
Paul Scott	1920–1978	India	*The Raj Quartet, Staying On*
Salman Rushdie	b. 1947	India and Pakistan	*Midnight's Children, Shame, The Satanic Verses*

Three other interesting contemporary English writers who, because of their parentage, have looked at English life from a slightly different perspective, are **Hanif Kureishi** (b. 1954), **Timothy Mo** (b. 1950) and **Kazuo Ishiguro** (b. 1954). Kureishi writes entertainingly about multi-racial London; two of his best-known works are the novel *The Buddha of Suburbia* (1990) and his script for the successful film, *My Beautiful Laundrette*, in 1985. Mo, born in Hong Kong, has written both about the Chinese community in London (*Sour Sweet*) and about his native Hong Kong during the British colonial period (*An Insular Possession*). Ishiguro has written a novel about Japan (*An Artist of the Floating World*) and a hugely successful one about England (*The Remains of the Day*); this was a fine study of a butler working for an upper-class gentleman in the period from the 1930s to the 1950s. The novel won the Booker Prize (see page 60), and was made into a successful film in 1993.

D H Lawrence

To return to earlier in the twentieth century and to another theme which has occupied a lot of space in English literature since then – sex. The man who brought to literature a new openness about this aspect of human relationships was one of the greatest of English novelists. **D H Lawrence** (1885–1930), who was from a poor mining family, first went into teaching, started writing poems, and then published his first novel *The White Peacock* in 1910. His first great achievement was *Sons and Lovers*, which introduced some of the themes which he would develop in his later work: provincial life, our response to nature and modern civilization, and sexuality. Several of Lawrence's novels were declared obscene and banned by the English authorities, and later his paintings (for Lawrence was also an artist) were similarly treated.

Lawrence's finest novels, *The Rainbow* and *Women in Love*, show his best qualities as a writer: his sensitivity, his ability to convey a sense of direct contact with life in all its aspects, and his wonderful poetic gift for describing human sensations and inner conflicts, as well as animals, flowers and landscapes. At his best, Lawrence is a true genius, and he certainly changed the way in which his successors could write about sexual relationships. Indeed, his last novel, *Lady Chatterley's Lover*, was banned in England, and could not be published until Penguin Books won a famous court case in 1961, allowing publication to go ahead.

The Bloomsbury Group

This was the name given to a group of English artists, novelists and other intellectuals who met in the Bloomsbury area of central London in the first quarter of the twentieth century. The only reason it is included in this section on the novel is because both E M Forster (mentioned earlier) and **Virginia Woolf** (1882–1941) were members. Virginia Woolf was one of the first to adopt the 'stream of consciousness' technique in the novel: every detail of a character's thoughts and impressions are recorded as they pass along the 'stream' of the mind, with the novelist able to control the order and structure in order to give the novel clarity and meaning. Though her novels – the best of which are perhaps *Mrs Dalloway*, *To the Lighthouse* and *Orlando* – are not to the taste of many readers today (some find her letters and journals more readable), Virginia Woolf is still seen as significant in helping to develop the art of the novel and as an early writer about feminist issues.

George Orwell

Unlike Virginia Woolf's, **Orwell**'s reputation is still as high today as it was when he was alive. He is also admired as an honest man with a strong social conscience. His name is largely associated with two famous novels, *Animal Farm* (1945) and *Nineteen Eighty-Four* (1949), but, excellent though these were, Orwell's achievements were far more than this. As a young man Orwell (whose real name was Eric Blair) joined the Imperial Police Force in Burma, where he spent five years. He then spent several years doing low jobs in Paris, and – wishing to see for himself the lives of the poorest people – living as a tramp in England; he used these experiences in his first book, *Down and Out in London and Paris*. Orwell went to Spain in 1936 to write as a journalist about the Spanish Civil War, but he soon joined the Republican army, and was wounded in battle. Two years later he wrote *Homage to Catalonia*, still one of the most useful books for those investigating that period of history.

Orwell then went on to write several novels and lots of essays and
journalism; during the Second World War he was pessimistic about
what the world might become after the conflict had finished.
Animal Farm, an allegory of the situation in Russia and the role of
Stalin during that time, met with huge success. So did *Nineteen
Eighty-Four* which took aspects of life in 1948 and projected these
into the future, a cruel vision of a world in which there is a loss of
individual freedom and total control by the state.

Graham Greene

Greene (1904–1991) was England's most popular novelist in the
middle period of the twentieth century. He divided his fiction into
two types: serious novels and those he called 'entertainments'. The
latter tended to be thrillers, featuring such elements as spies,
betrayal, and inner struggles of heroes who are trying to distinguish
between good and evil. Examples of his 'entertainments' are *A Gun
for Sale, The Ministry of Fear, Our Man in Havana,* and, best of all
perhaps, *The Third Man* (in 1949 he wrote the script for this film –
which in 1999 was voted by critics the best ever British film – and
then wrote the short story in 1950). The moral dilemmas which
these entertainments touched on were more seriously described in
his other novels, the best of which come from his mid-career:
Brighton Rock, The Power and the Glory, The Heart of the Matter
and *The End of the Affair.* The fact that Greene was an increasingly
uneasy Catholic clearly had an influence on his work: his main
characters are always worried about the morality of their actions.
The world he creates ('Greeneland', as it has been called) is
generally one of corruption, pain and despair – yet his novels
remain very enjoyable to read. One critic amusingly found that if
you shorten the pronunciation of 'Graham Greene', you get 'Grim
Grin', which seems very suitable for the kind of reaction his novels
produce!

William Golding

Golding (1911–1993) was the last English writer to win the Nobel
Prize for Literature (in 1983). He was a teacher for several years,
and his first novel, *Lord of the Flies* (1954), uses that experience in
a surprising way. The novel is about a group of English schoolboys

who, after a plane crash, have to live on a desert island; the group soon divides, and descends into violence. Golding is interested in how the boys behave when they are 'free' with no adults to control or guide them, and, on another level, he examines the thin line between civilization and anarchy. Golding's other novels are also dramatic moral tales, often with the sea as background: the best are *Pincher Martin,* about a drowning sailor, *The Spire,* which has as its theme the building of a cathedral, and the novel for which he won the Booker Prize in 1980, *Rites of Passage,* set on a ship heading for Australia at the beginning of the nineteenth century.

The novel today

Out of the rich variety of contemporary fiction, 'airport' novels are probably the best-sellers. These novels are not about airports, but are the type of book bought by those about to go away on holiday. They are often thick thrillers by English writers such as **Robert Goddard**, **Ken Follett** or **Frederick Forsyth**; romances by **Catherine Cookson**, **Jilly Cooper** or **Rosamunde Pilcher**; or part of a fashion which has been called 'chicklit', that is humorous stories – written by women – about young, working, unmarried women who live fairly unhappy lives full of wine, cigarettes and unsuccessful love affairs (*The Diary of Bridget Jones* by **Helen Fielding** being the classic example).

However, if you are looking for current English novelists whose work is likely to last and to be considered the best of this age, here is a brief selection (to which should be added the names of **Timothy Mo**, **Hanif Kureishi** and **Kazuo Ishiguro**; see page 56).

Author	Dates	Best novels
Angela Carter	1940–1992	*The Magic Toyshop, Nights at the Circus, Wise Children*
Pat Barker	b. 1943	*Union Street, The Regeneration Trilogy*
Ian McEwan	b. 1948	*In Between the Sheets, Enduring Love, Atonement*

Martin Amis	b. 1949	*Money, London Fields, Time's Arrow*
Julian Barnes	b. 1949	*Flaubert's Parrot, Cross-Channel, England, England*
Louis de Bernières	b. 1954	*The Troublesome Offspring of Cardinal Guzman, Captain Corelli's Mandolin*
Nick Hornby	b. 1957	*Fever Pitch, High Fidelity, About A Boy, How to be Good*

Literary prizes

Such prizes have been around a long while now: Rudyard Kipling was the first Englishman to win the Nobel Prize for Literature (1907), and V S Naipaul (who lives in England but was born in the Caribbean) the most recent (2001). The Booker Prize, which was first awarded in 1969, has grown into the most important literary event of the year. It is given to the best novel of the year and is currently worth £50,000 to the winner. Previous winners include some of England's best: Paul Scott, Iris Murdoch, Kingsley Amis, Pat Barker and Ian McEwan. There are, of course, many other less well-known awards – for poetry, plays, first novels, crime novels, children's fiction and Commonwealth writers. Some are sponsored by newspapers (for example, *The Guardian* Fiction Prize), others by institutions or companies.

Special strengths

English literature can also claim several other areas which have produced memorable work which is famous throughout the world.

Children's literature

Perhaps there is something gentle and whimsical in the English character which makes it good at producing books with characters and situations which appeal to children (and adults too!). Did your parents read you any of these when you were a child? Have you read them yourself, or have you read them to your own children?

Tom Brown's Schooldays (1857) by Thomas Hughes
Alice's Adventures in Wonderland (1865) by Lewis Carroll
Black Beauty (1877) by Anna Sewell
Treasure Island (1883) by R L Stevenson
The Tale of Peter Rabbit (1893) by Beatrix Potter
The Jungle Book (1894) by Rudyard Kipling
The Railway Children (1906) by E Nesbit
The Wind in the Willows (1908) by Kenneth Grahame
The Secret Garden (1911) by Frances Hodgson Burnett
The Young Visiters (1919) by Daisy Ashford
Dr Dolittle (1920) by Hugh Lofting
Just William (1922) by Richmal Crompton
Winnie-the-Pooh (1926) by A A Milne
Little Grey Rabbit (1929) by Alison Uttley
Swallows and Amazons (1930) by Arthur Ransome
National Velvet (1935) by Enid Bagnold
Ballet Shoes (1936) by Noel Streatfeild
The Hobbit (1937) by J R R Tolkien

Several of the books in the list (eg *The Tale of Peter Rabbit, Just William, Swallows and Amazons* and Noel Streatfeild's ballet stories) began series which went on to become hugely popular. This was an impressive list even before the strong development of children's literature in the years after the Second World War. Since then, the great names in this field have been **C S Lewis** (1898–1963), **Roald Dahl** (1916–1990) and **J K Rowling** (b. 1965). Their big successes have been:

Lewis	The seven novels of *The Chronicles of Narnia*
Dahl	*Charlie and the Chocolate Factory, Fantastic Mr Fox, The Twits, The BFG, Matilda*, etc
Rowling	The *Harry Potter* novels (with more books – and films – to come...)

Detective stories

It is said that the English invented this genre, with Wilkie Collins' novel, *The Moonstone*, in 1868. Over the years, English writers have developed the 'whodunit', as this type of fiction is sometimes called (ie who dun – or *did*, in correct English! – the murder?), into a fine art. This is perhaps understandable in a country where so many people enjoy crosswords, puzzles and quizzes. Two names above all stand out in this genre: **Conan Doyle** (the Scot who created Sherlock Holmes) and **Agatha Christie** (1890–1976). Agatha Christie wrote her first detective novel in 1920, and went on to produce sixty-five more, as well as several plays, one of which, *The Mousetrap*, has been running continuously in a London theatre since 1952. Several of her novels have been made into films, and two of her detectives, Hercule Poirot and Miss Marple, have appeared in popular TV adaptations of the novels. You do not read Agatha Christie's books for the wonderful characters or the beautiful style, you read them for the brilliant plots and the way in which she can so cleverly lead you, the reader, into making false assumptions about 'whodunit'. Other great names in English detective fiction are:

Writer	Dates	Crime-solvers
G K Chesterton	1874 – 1936	Father Brown
Dorothy Sayers	1893 – 1957	Lord Peter Wimsey
P D James	b. 1920	Delia Gray, Adam Dalgleish
Ruth Rendell/ Barbara Vine	b. 1930	Inspector Wexford
Colin Dexter	b. 1930	Inspector Morse

Spy thrillers

This genre began in the 1930s as a variation from detective fiction: as already mentioned, Graham Greene wrote several novels of this type, as did **Eric Ambler** (1909–1998) whose gripping novels usually tell the story of an innocent Englishman involved in murder and intrigue in Southern Europe. Strongly recommended are *The Dark Frontier, The Mask of Dimitrios* and *Doctor Frigo*. And so we come to the creator of James Bond, **Ian Fleming** (1908–1964): his tough, clever and sophisticated hero first appeared in *Casino Royale* in 1952. (The first of the hugely successful series of Bond films was *Dr No* in 1962.) Fleming wrote twelve Bond novels in all: the secret of their success – and of the films – lies in the clever mixture of exotic locations, sex, violence, technology (all those special cars and weapons!) and wit.

A more serious writer about the morality of spies, spying and the whole struggle between good and evil is **John Le Carré** (b. 1931). His best-known novel, *The Spy Who Came in from the Cold*, was set in Berlin, and had as its background the Cold War and its effect on individuals. Le Carré also created the character of George Smiley, the quiet secret agent who appears in many of his later novels and in the many TV adaptations of these stories. Other recommended novels by Le Carré are *A Small Town in Germany, Tinker Tailor Soldier Spy,* and *The Little Drummer-Girl.*

Science fiction

While spy stories have become less common, science fiction has risen in popularity. This genre is also English in origin, but owes its creation partly to the Frenchman, **Jules Verne**, who in the 1860s wrote adventure stories with unusual settings, as in *Journey to the Centre of the Earth* and *Twenty Thousand Leagues Under the Sea.* **H G Wells** (1866–1946) built on this and was the first to write fiction using the scientific advances of his time in novels such as *The Time Machine, The War of the Worlds,* and *The First Men on the Moon.* Until the Second World War, science fiction stories involved fantastic adventures and machines, but since then the genre has developed to include political, technological and even philosophical themes which, though set in the future, suggest the worries of today. Many well-known novelists (eg Huxley, Orwell, K Amis and Doris Lessing) have written works of science fiction as well as the novels for which they are best known. Today, the specialist English writers of science fiction (or 'Sci Fi' as it is commonly known) are **Brian Aldiss**, **J G Ballard**, **Arthur C Clarke**, **Michael Moorcock** and **Terry Pratchett**.

Comic writing

Let us end this chapter on a lighter note. The English are known throughout the world for having a 'special' sense of humour, and certainly English literature contains plenty of evidence of this. 'Taking it further' will suggest some more good sources, but meanwhile here are a few comic highlights, starting with limericks (a type of amusing poem which the English invented in the eighteenth century: it has a fixed five-line pattern, with the 'twist' in the last line). Limericks are still popular today, and some of them can be very rude – but not this one!

There was a young lady of Riga,
Who rode with a smile on a tiger,
They returned from the ride
With the lady inside
And the smile on the face of the tiger.

Comic creators and their creations		
Writer	**Dates**	**Best books**
Thomas Love Peacock	1785–1866	*Headlong Hall, Nightmare Abbey*
Edward Lear	1812–1888	*A Book of Nonsense,* *Laughable Lyrics*
Lewis Carroll	1832–1898	*Alice's Adventures in Wonderland,* *Through the Looking-Glass*
George and Weedon Grossmith	1847–1912 1854–1919	*Diary of a Nobody*
Jerome K Jerome	1859–1927	*Three Men in a Boat*
Hilaire Belloc	1870–1953	*The Bad Child's Book of Beasts,* *Cautionary Tales*
P G Wodehouse	1881–1975	*Leave it to Psmith, Carry on* *Jeeves, The Code of the* *Woosters, Hot Water,* *Laughing Gas*
Evelyn Waugh	1903–1966	*Decline and Fall, Vile Bodies,* *A Handful of Dust, Scoop,* *Brideshead Revisited*
Kingsley Amis	1922–1995	*Lucky Jim, Take A Girl Like You,* *One Fat Englishman, Jake's Thing*
Tom Sharpe	b. 1928	*Porterhouse Blue, Wilt*
David Lodge	b. 1935	*Changing Places, Small World,* *Nice Work*

So, with the sound of laughter, we come to the end of our short tour of the lovely orchard of English literature. If you would like to try some more of its fruits, read on...

GLOSSARY

absurdist type of play in the 1950s and 1960s which rejected logic and reason in trying to show or explain the human condition

allegory story in which the characters and events are meant to represent other ideas

anthology collection in a book, of chosen poems, stories, etc

Dadaist follower of the Dada movement in art and literature which tried to shock people into thinking again about the meaning of art

epigram short phrase which says something wise and witty

farce characters involved in funny and unlikely situations

genre a type or style of art, literature or music with its own special features

gossip columns sections of newspapers that deal with the private lives of famous people

intrigue secret plans often by or against foreign governments

melancholy strong feeling of sadness which affects one's attitude to life

menacing suggesting that danger or harm is likely to happen

narrator teller of a story

obscene dealing with sex in a way that is likely to upset people

ode poem in praise of someone or some event

opium powerful drug, once used as a medicine, made from the seeds of the poppy flower

sonnet poem of fourteen lines, some of which rhyme

tramp person with no home or job who travels around the country

trilogy three-part work (eg books or films)

visionary someone who has visions of the future of a religious nature

whimsical charming and amusing but in a slightly annoying way

Taking it further

Suggested reading

Reference books:

Scott-Kilvert (ed), *British Writers*, volumes 1–7, The British Council, 1994

Drabble (ed), *The Oxford Companion to English Literature*, 2000

Carpenter and Prichard (eds), *The Oxford Companion to Children's Literature*, OUP, 1994

Modern English poets:

Wendy Cope, *Making Cocoa for Kingsley Amis* and *Serious Concerns*

Fred D'Aguiar, *Bloodlines* and *An English Sampler*

John Hegley, *Five Sugars Please* and *Glad to Wear Glasses*

Benjamin Zephaniah, *City Psalms* and *Too Black, Too Strong*

Modern playwrights:

Caryl Churchill, *Top Girls* and *Serious Money*

David Hare, *Plenty* and *Racing Demon*

Patrick Marber, *Dealer's Choice* and *Closer*

Modern novelists:

A S Byatt, *The Virgin in the Garden* and *Possession*

Graham Swift, *Waterland* and *Last Orders*

Jeanette Winterson, *Oranges are not the only Fruit* and *Written on the Body*

Modern writers for children/ teenagers:

Melvin Burgess, *Junk* and *Kite*

Anne Fine, *Madame Doubtfire* and *Very Different*

Alan Garner, *Red Shift* and *The Owl Service*

Philip Pullman, the *Dark Materials* trilogy

Robert Westall, *Stormsearch* and *The Machine Gunners*

Newspaper:

The Times Literary Supplement (a weekly newspaper)

Websites

http://www.books.guardian.co.uk/authors

http://www.lion.chadwyck.co.uk   A database, run by Oxford University, of English and American literature with links to other Web resources

http://www.bartleby.com/cambridge   The Cambridge history of English and American literature

http://www.britishtheatre.about.com

http://www.britishliterature.com

Places to visit

Westminster Abbey in London, where many of the greatest English writers are buried.

Writers' houses (often kept as museums dedicated to the writers):

Shakespeare's in Stratford-upon-Avon
Keats' in Hampstead, North London
Dickens' in Doughty Street, London
Penshurst Place in Kent (Sir Philip Sidney)
Lamb House in Rye, Sussex (Henry James)
Kipling's house in Burwash, Sussex
the Wordsworths' cottage in Grasmere, the Lake District
the Brontë sisters' home in Haworth, Yorkshire.

4 ART AND ARCHITECTURE

To anyone investigating the story of English art, the first puzzle that arises is that there are so few books on the subject. This seems to be partly due to a belief among some English people that there have been very few great English artists, but we shall try to show you here that this is not the case. Nikolaus Pevsner, the German-born commentator on English art, wrote in *The Englishness of English Art*: 'None of the other nations of Europe has so abject an inferiority complex about its own aesthetic capabilities as England'. Throughout the ages, English art and architecture have almost always had a distinctive character of their own and there have been some remarkable achievements in both fields. In art, the names of Constable, Turner, Gainsborough, Whistler, Bacon, Spencer and Freud stand out, while in architecture we have, amongst others, Wren, Nash, Pugin, Foster, Rogers and Grimshaw, all of whom developed their own individual styles. Nor should we forget the creators of English domestic architecture, who have given the towns and villages of England an appearance and an atmosphere that is distinctively English. The decorative arts also have given us fine works, in china and pottery, furniture and interior design. Finally, in the twentieth century England produced some of the world's great sculptors.

Early architecture

Very little survives from before the Norman Conquest. The great circle of standing stones at Stonehenge in Wiltshire was built about four thousand years ago, possibly for some religious purpose, though nobody really knows why. The inner circle was made with stones, each weighing up to 4 tons, from the Preseli Mountains in the west of Wales, about 240 miles (360 km) away; while the stones of the outer circle – some weighing as much as 50 tons – came from the Marlborough Downs, 20 miles (32 km) away. We can only try to guess how the builders transported these great stones, but it was an extraordinary achievement. Roman ruins are scattered all over the country – villas, forts, public baths and town walls. One of the best preserved is Hadrian's Wall, stretching across the country from coast to coast and built to mark the most northerly extent of the Roman empire. A few small Saxon churches can also still be found, with round arches and square towers, for example, the Chuch of St Laurence at Bradford-on-Avon. In some cases the church was later rebuilt, leaving only the original Saxon crypt.

From the Middle Ages to the Reformation

Medieval English churches look very different today from how they would have looked before the time of Henry VIII. In the Middle Ages, their interiors would have been richly decorated with colourful statues, murals and paintings. When Henry VIII established the Church of England and ordered the dissolution of the monasteries in 1536, he started an extraordinary process of artistic destruction. Over the next hundred and twenty years, until the death of Cromwell in 1658, almost all religious art was systematically destroyed. Church walls were whitewashed, stone statues were defaced or smashed to pieces, and paintings were burnt. Bishop Latimer, for example, collected wooden statues from all over the country and burned them on huge bonfires in London. As a result, we have relatively little art from this period to see today. A few paintings and other small works of art were hidden and survived. The exquisite Wilton Diptych was painted for King Richard II, and shows him kneeling with three saints before the Virgin Mary who is holding the infant Jesus and surrounded by angels. It can be seen in the Sainsbury Wing of the National Gallery in London.

In architecture, the story is somewhat different. It is true that a good many fine religious buildings were destroyed during the Reformation. The King's men took the treasure of Fountains Abbey by force, and Tintern Abbey was stripped of its lead roof and stained glass; similar destruction occurred throughout England. However, the majority of religious buildings were simply taken over, and many medieval churches still survive, giving English villages their characteristic appearance.

Norman architecture

The ruling Norman aristocracy had been relatively few in number, and protected themselves by building thick-walled stone castles, many of which can still be seen. Dover Castle is well-preserved and stands high above the white cliffs, while the massive keep of the Tower of London is one of London's most famous landmarks. The Normans also built massive cathedrals with long naves, thick columns and carved round arches which are so characteristic of Norman architecture. Norwich and Durham cathedrals are fine examples from this period. Much of the earliest work was designed and carried out by builders and stonemasons imported from Normandy.

English Gothic

Gradually a more English style developed, though influenced by the Gothic style becoming popular in much of the rest of northern Europe. Round arches became pointed, there were more and larger windows, and roof vaults became more complex. English Gothic is divided into three phases:

- **Early English**, characterized by pointed arches and flying buttresses. Good examples include Salisbury Cathedral and Lincoln Cathedral.
- **Decorated**, whose features include windows with delicate stonework patterns, and elaborate stone carving, usually of leaves and flowers, especially on capitals. Exeter Cathedral, Wells Cathedral, and the Chapter House of York Minster all exemplify the Decorated style.
- **Perpendicular**, a style that remained influential for two hundred years (1350–1550) and used greatly enlarged windows, flatter arches and fan vaults in the roof. Gloucester Cathedral and King's College Chapel, Cambridge were both built in the Perpendicular style.

Fan vaulting at King's College Chapel, Cambridge

The Renaissance

Portraiture

Since Henry VIII had effectively banned religious art, the subjects that were allowed to be painted were very limited, though miniature portraits were very popular and remained so for the next two or three hundred years. **Nicholas Hilliard** (1547–1619), painting in the time of Elizabeth I, was one of the most accomplished painters of miniatures. Examples of his work can be seen in the National Portrait Gallery in London. Larger portraits also became fashionable, but most of the artists who produced these were foreigners, especially Dutch and Flemish, who were commissioned by members of the aristocracy. Since statues of religious figures were no longer allowed in churches, sculpture was also limited during this period, mainly to the decoration of tombs.

Great houses

Architecture was increasingly influenced by classical Italian design, sometimes directly from Italy, but mostly via France or the Netherlands because the Reformation had cut the previously close links with Rome. The wealthy and powerful no longer felt they needed to live in fortified castles, and England's increasing prosperity meant that there were many successful merchants and members of the nobility who could afford grand country houses. Most of these great houses continued to have a large central hall, just like the fortified manor houses of medieval times, but with many additional rooms usually laid out in a symmetrical arrangement, and surrounded by elegant gardens. Glass was very expensive at this time, and one way a rich landowner could display his wealth was by building a mansion with many large windows. Some of the best examples are Hardwick Hall in Derbyshire, Longleat House in Wiltshire, or perhaps the grandest mansion of the time, Burghley House in Northamptonshire.

The seventeenth and eighteenth centuries

During the reign of James I, Jacobean architecture was similar in many ways to the Elizabethan style of the late sixteenth century but with more classical features. The influence of classical architecture grew stronger, in particular through the work of **Inigo Jones** (1573–1652). According to David Watkin's *English Architecture*, 'The revolution effected in English architecture by Inigo Jones was important not merely for establishing a change of style, but also a change in the intellectual and social status of the designer of buildings'. Architecture as a profession in England had begun. Until that time it had usually been the hobby of the rich.

Palladian style

Inigo Jones, like many after him, travelled to Italy and spent many years there as a young man studying Italian art and architecture before returning to England. He was particularly influenced by the Italian architect Andrea Palladio, and in the 1620s introduced the Palladian style to England. This style looked back to the principles of classical architecture which governed the correct proportions of height and width. At the time (the early seventeenth century), Jones' work was regarded as rather strange, and only a few of his buildings survive today, including the Queen's House at Greenwich and the Banqueting House in Whitehall, London.

English Baroque

The Great Fire of London in 1666 destroyed St Paul's Cathedral, dozens of churches and thousands of houses in the City of London. The astronomer **Christopher Wren** (1632–1723) had become more and more interested in architecture, and he immediately suggested a grand scheme to rebuild the city with wide, straight streets, massive public buildings and large squares. His plan was not adopted, but he was commissioned to design the new St Paul's Cathedral, as well as a large number of churches. St Paul's took more than thirty-five years to complete, and its great dome still dominates the city's skyline today. Wren's style was essentially Baroque but with an English touch, and in this he was followed by **John Vanbrugh** (1664–1726), the architect of Blenheim Palace for the first Duke of Marlborough. Vanbrugh worked with a pupil of Wren's, **Nicholas Hawksmoor** (1661–1736), whose finest work is the six London churches he designed between 1712 and 1716, and which survive to this day. **James Gibbs** (1682–1754) continued the development of English Baroque with the design of churches like St Martin-in-the-Fields in Trafalgar Square, and the splendid circular domed library of Oxford University, the Radcliffe Camera.

Classical style

Nearly a hundred years after Inigo Jones had introduced Palladianism, it was revived by **Lord Burlington** (1694–1753), **Colen Campbell** (d. 1729) and **William Kent** (1685–1748) in the early eighteenth century in a deliberate attempt to replace the Baroque style with a simpler style based on classical principles. Characteristic features of the style include a portico with six columns. Chiswick House in West London and Holkham Hall in Norfolk are striking examples of the Palladian style. Classical style remained the dominant influence in architecture throughout the eighteenth century, though more flexibly interpreted in the highly individual work of **Sir John Soane** (1753–1837).

From portraiture to landscape painting

The seventeenth century was not, on the whole, a great period for native English artists; the most famous painters working in

England at the time, such as Rubens, Van Dyck and Lely, were all foreign-born. The tradition of miniature portrait painting was, however, continued by artists such as **Samuel Cooper** (1609–1672), who was asked by Oliver Cromwell to paint him exactly as he was, 'warts and all'. The result is a fine and extraordinarily realistic portrait.

The great English painter of the early eighteenth century was **William Hogarth** (1697–1764). He broke away from the long tradition of portraiture, and developed his own satirical style, telling a story with a moral in a series of paintings. His *Rake's Progress*, which can be seen in the Soane Museum in London, is one of his best-known works. The second half of the eighteenth century is dominated by two great portraitists, **Joshua Reynolds** (1723–1792) and **Thomas Gainsborough** (1727–1788). Reynolds was born in Devon, in the West Country, but moved to London to study painting. In 1749 he travelled to Italy. He stayed there for four years, and was profoundly influenced by all he saw, but especially by Michelangelo's paintings on the ceiling of the Sistine Chapel. He later became the first president of the Royal Academy of Arts, and encouraged young artists to study the great masters of the past. The majority of his paintings were portraits, with his sitters often posing in scenes from classical mythology. Gainsborough, too, is mainly known for his portraits such as *Mrs Siddons* (now in the National Gallery in London), but he was also an accomplished landscape painter. Landscape painting is a genre in which English artists have particularly excelled.

Another outstanding, but often overlooked, artist of the eighteenth century was **George Stubbs** (1724–1806). He first studied anatomy and then specialized in sporting pictures, usually of horses.

The nineteenth century

Landscape painting was hugely popular in the nineteenth century, the two great artists of this genre being **John Constable** (1776–1837) and **J M W Turner** (1775–1851). Their styles were totally different. Constable concentrated on idyllic English scenes of rural life, with trees, fields, and streams reflecting the light of the sky. There is an extraordinary sense of movement in his painting of clouds. Turner, unlike Constable, travelled abroad and this is reflected in his many paintings of Italy, especially Venice, and the Alps. His paintings of the sea, another favourite theme, convey the tremendous forces of nature. He worked with both watercolours and oils, and much of his work was highly experimental and often not well understood or appreciated at the time.

The Pre-Raphaelites

The Pre-Raphaelite Brotherhood was formed in 1848 by **William Holman Hunt** (1827–1910), **Dante Gabriel Rossetti** (1828–1882) and **John Everett Millais** (1829–1896). As the name suggests, they intended to revive the style of fifteenth century Italian art, before the time of Raphael, a kind of escape from the reality of industrial England to some purer past. They were later joined by **Edward Burne-Jones** (1833–1898) and **Ford Madox Brown** (1821–1893).

Regency architecture

Early nineteenth-century architecture was neo-classical in style, and is generally referred to as Regency. **Decimus Burton** (1800–1881), **Henry Holland** (1745–1806), and **John Nash** (1752–1835) are associated with this style. A good example can be found in the grand terraces of houses designed by Nash around Regent's Park in London. Regency style was also influenced by a fashion for the oriental, the supreme example of which is the extraordinary Royal Pavilion that Nash built at Brighton for George IV while he was still Prince Regent.

The Gothic Revival

The Pre-Raphaelites had been influenced by the writer and philosopher John Ruskin, who supported a reaction against the classical style in English architecture, promoting instead a revival of traditional styles, especially Gothic, and the use of traditional building materials such as brick which had long ago been replaced by stone in the design of great houses and public buildings. The architect and interior designer **Augustus Pugin** (1817–1852) was also enormously influential in the Gothic Revival, declaring that Gothic architecture was 'not a style, but a principle'. While

Charles Barry (1795–1860) designed the new Houses of Parliament, after the old Palace of Westminster had burned down in 1834, Pugin designed the interiors. Started in 1840, the building took more than twenty years to complete, and it remains the finest example of early Victorian Gothic. The classical style influenced by Italy continued to find some support especially amongst Liberal politicians, while the Gothic Revival was favoured by Conservatives. The so-called 'Battle of the Styles' continued through the middle of the nineteenth century and resulted in the compromise style of the buildings of the South Kensington cultural complex in London, including the Victoria and Albert Museum, the Royal Albert Hall and the Natural History Museum, which all contain elements of both Italianate and Gothic styles. Gothic remained popular in a variety of forms throughout the Victorian era; notable architects include **Alfred Waterhouse** (1873–1881), **George Gilbert Scott** (1811–1878), and **William Butterfield** (1814–1900).

The Crystal Palace

Alongside the revival of more traditional building materials, there was also a good deal of experimentation with new ones, and with novel ways of heating and ventilating large buildings. The Crystal Palace, designed by **Joseph Paxton** (1801–1865), must have been an extraordinary sight. It was a massive construction of iron and glass built in Hyde Park for the Great Exhibition of 1851. After the Exhibition it was dismantled and re-erected in Sydenham, South London. Sadly it was destroyed in a fire in 1936, but it has given its name to the area of South London where it was located, and to a local football club.

Late Victorian architecture

The greatest architect of the late Victorian era was probably **Richard Norman Shaw** (1831–1912) who designed in a variety of styles, including 'Old English' strongly influenced by medieval houses, with tall brick chimneys and leaded windows, and 'Queen Anne', reminiscent of the late seventeenth- and early eighteenth-century styles.

The early twentieth century

One of the most distinctive architects of the late nineteenth and early twentieth centuries was **Sir Edwin Lutyens** (1869–1944). Most of his work was domestic, and he made use of local materials. His style was influenced by the Arts and Crafts Movement, looking back as it did to medieval times, but was simplified and modernized to take account of contemporary tastes. (See the section below on the decorative arts for more information on the Arts and Crafts Movement). Lutyens had a long and very successful partnership with the garden designer **Gertrude Jekyll** (1843–1932).

While modernism flourished in Europe, it made relatively little impact on either art or architecture in England for at least the first thirty years of the twentieth century. **Walter Sickert** (1860–1942) was perhaps the best known of a group of painters in the early years of the twentieth century known as the Camden Town group. The group also included **Spencer Gore** (1878–1914) and **Harold Gilman** (1876–1919).

In sculpture, **Jacob Epstein** (1880–1959) was the pre-eminent figure in the first decade or so of the twentieth century. His nude figures for the façade of the new headquarters of the British Medical Association in the Strand, London, finished in 1908, caused a public outcry on the grounds that they were obscene, and they were eventually destroyed. **Henry Moore** (1898–1986), like Epstein, was strongly influenced by non-European art, especially from Africa and Latin America. He is probably best known for his giant reclining female figures, a recurring theme in his work. **Barbara Hepworth** (1903–1975) and her husband **Ben Nicholson** (1894–1982), who was also an abstract painter, worked as sculptors in a colony of artists in St Ives, Cornwall, establishing an international reputation.

From the Second World War to the present day

Until his death, **Francis Bacon** (1909–1992) was considered one of the world's greatest living artists. He was not formally trained as an artist, but his first exhibition in 1945 of *Three Studies for*

Figures at the Base of a Crucifixion (now in the Tate Gallery) caused a sensation. His style was Expressionist, and his images – often of distorted human figures – are deeply disturbing. He is reported to have said, 'Painting is the pattern of one's own nervous system being projected on the canvas.' His friend **Graham Sutherland** (1903–1980) was renowned for his portraits, landscapes and still lifes. One of Sutherland's best-known works is the huge tapestry portraying Christ in Coventry Cathedral. **Stanley Spencer** (1891–1959), whose Surrealist work dealt mainly with religious themes was another prominent name in post-war English art. The Pop Art movement began in England in 1954 as a response to commercial culture. Its most famous exponent is **David Hockney** (b. 1937).

BritArt

English art since about 1980 or so defies classification. It has made use of a variety of different media, often mixed in the same work. Much of it seems to be preoccupied with death and decay. One of the best-known of recent English artists is **Damien Hirst** (b. 1965), whose work has included medicine cabinets and whole or sliced animals pickled in formaldehyde and displayed in glass cases. While still a student he had the idea for an exhibition called Freeze, which he organized and which displayed some of his own work as well as that of several of his fellow students at Goldsmiths College in London. This is often regarded as the beginning of 'BritArt', the emergence of a group of Young British Artists (YBAs) who put on their own shows, and were clever at promoting themselves through the media. Another of these artists is **Tracy Emin** (b. 1963), famous for her dirty, unmade bed which was shortlisted for the Turner Prize in 1999.

The Turner Prize

The Turner Prize almost always provokes controversy. It is awarded annually by the Tate Gallery to the British artist who has produced the most outstanding work in the previous twelve months. Nominations come from the general public as well as the jury. In 1993 the prize was won by Rachel Whiteread

(b. 1963) for *House*. Whiteread filled a small terraced London house with concrete, then stripped away the mould – the house itself – leaving something like a ghost of the house. **Damien Hirst** won in 1995, while in 1997 the winner was **Gillian Wearing** (b. 1963) with a video called *Sixty Minute Silence*. In 1998, **Chris Ofili** (b. 1968) won the prize with a picture of the Virgin Mary created with paper collage, oil paint, glitter and elephant dung on a linen base.

Modern architecture

The Modern Movement in architecture had little impact in England until the 1950s, with the building of the Royal Festival Hall in London, and Coventry Cathedral designed by **Sir Basil Spence** (1907–1976). Both buildings were more popular with the general public than with other architects. The use of concrete led to a style known as the New Brutalism, exemplified by the stark concrete terraces of the National Theatre (1967–1976) on London's South Bank. More recent architects have experimented with a

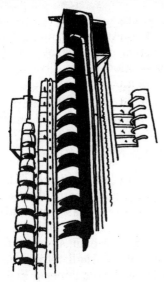

range of modern materials to dramatic effect. They include **Norman Foster** (b. 1935) – the Great Court at the British Museum, and Stansted Airport, Essex; **Richard Rogers** (b. 1933) – the Reuters and Lloyds Buildings in London; and **Nicholas Grimshaw** (b. 1939) – the Financial Times Printing Works, and the International Terminal at Waterloo Station. While post-modern architects have made greater use of colour and texture, architects such as **Quinlan Terry** (b. 1937) have developed a new Classical style to complement existing older buildings.

The Lloyds Building

Domestic architecture through the ages

Older houses in English towns and villages are generally built of local materials, and these tend to produce a distinctive local style. Timber has always been widely available, and many of the oldest surviving houses are timber-framed. Thatch, made from straw or reeds, was once the commonest type of roof but went out of fashion because it was associated with the homes of the poorest people. It can still be seen in some villages, especially in the south and east of England, where thatched roofs are preserved as a rural tradition. In the north and west of England, a wide variety of different types of stone suitable for building are found, giving the villages of the Cotswolds, Cumbria, and Devon their distinctive character and charm.

Flats have never been as popular in England as they are in the rest of Europe, except in the centre of larger towns and cities; housing in the suburbs consists mainly of two- or three-storey houses, in terraces, semi-detached, or detached. A garden, however small, is regarded as essential. Current styles of house building, as so often before in England, look back to the past. This preference for houses and gardens has, of course, led to large areas of former countryside being swallowed up by 'urban sprawl', and there is now growing interest in the better use of urban space for new housing developments. Riverside apartment blocks are growing in popularity, especially those with balconies and river views; and derelict warehouses in dockland areas are being converted into modern flats.

The decorative arts

For at least the last two or three hundred years, England has been renowned for its applied arts. In the eighteenth century, three great cabinet-makers – **Sheraton**, **Hepplewhite** and **Chippendale** – produced furniture of exquisite beauty. It was light and delicate, with slender legs, and made use of inlaid or painted decoration. This period too saw the development of the English tradition of fine ceramic art. **Josiah Wedgwood** was the pre-eminent English potter of his day, and he created the distinctive jasperware – hard, unglazed pottery, especially vases, usually blue, and decorated with delicate white figures in relief – which the company he founded still produces today. Other famous makers of china and pottery include **Minton, Doulton** and **Staffordshire**.

The Arts and Crafts Movement developed out of the Gothic Revival in the nineteenth century with its concern for high quality craftsmanship and the use of traditional building materials. **William Morris** (1834–1896) was a socialist who imagined an ideal society where people no longer worked in ugly factories, turning out poor quality mass-produced goods, but worked instead as skilled artisans. He set up his own interior design company, producing textiles, wallpaper, furniture and stained glass; many of his designs are still popular today.

GLOSSARY

capital top part of a column or pillar

crypt room under a church

dissolution (from the verb 'to dissolve') closure of the monasteries

flying buttress a buttress is a stone support built against a wall; a flying buttress is one that is separate from the wall it supports, but connected to it by an arch

genre category of works of art with a common form or subject

keep main fortified tower of a castle

landscape painting showing a view of scenery in the countryside

mural large picture painted directly onto a wall

nave long central part of a church where people usually sit

portrait painting of a person; a '*portraitist*' is a painter of portraits, and '*portraiture*' is the art of painting portraits

relief decoration that stands out from a flat surface

still life painting of an arrangement of non-living objects

vault arched ceiling; fan vaults have curved stone ribs like the ribs of a fan

Taking it further

Suggested reading

Watkin, David, *English Architecture*, Thames and Hudson, 2001
Graham-Dixon, Andrew, *A History of British Art*, BBC Books,
    1996
Quiney, Anthony, *The Traditional Buildings of England*, Thames
    and Hudson, 1990
Pevsner, Nikolaus, *The Englishness of English Art*, Penguin
    Books, 1964

Places to visit

The most comprehensive collection of English art can be seen at
the **Tate Britain** gallery at Millbank, London. The nearest
underground station is Pimlico on the Victoria Line, or it is a short
walk from the Houses of Parliament. The entire collection can be
seen online; just visit the Tate's website (see below).

The **National Gallery** in Trafalgar Square, London, has a more
international collection, but it also contains a good many fine
English paintings. Its collection, too, can be seen online (see
below). The **National Portrait Gallery** is next door to the National
Gallery.

The **National Trust** now owns and manages many of the grand
country houses built through the ages, and these are open to the
public. For a complete list of National Trust properties, have a look
at their website (see below).

The **Wallace Collection**, one of the less well-known galleries in
London, has a substantial number of paintings by Joshua Reynolds.
It is in Hertford House, Manchester Square, not far from Oxford
Street.

Gainsborough's House in Sudbury, Suffolk, is the birthplace of
Thomas Gainsborough and houses the largest collection of his
work in the country.

Nostell Priory in Yorkshire is a Palladian mansion belonging to the
National Trust with a fine collection of Chippendale furniture.

The city of **Bath** has many examples of fine classical architecture, for example, The Circus, Great Pulteney Street, Pulteney Bridge and The Royal Crescent.

Sir John Soane's Museum in Lincoln's Inn Fields, London, is also the house that Soane designed for himself, and contains his collections and personal effects.

The **William Morris Gallery** in Walthamstow has a comprehensive collection of his work.

Websites

The Tate Britain: **http://www.tate.org.uk/britain/default.htm**
The National Gallery:
   http://www.nationalgallery.org.uk/collection/default.htm
The National Trust: **http://www.nationaltrust.org.uk/**
The Wallace Collection:
   http://www.the-wallace-collection.org.uk/
Gainsborough's House: **http://www.gainsborough.org/**
Sir John Soane's Museum: **http://www.soane.org/**
The William Morris Gallery:
   http://www.lbwf.gov.uk/wmg/home.htm

5 | MUSIC

If you were to ask anyone, from an Australian to an Icelander, what names they think of when you say the words, 'English music', it is almost certain that the first name on their lips would be that of a pop star (The Beatles, Elton John, George Michael, the Spice Girls...). Indeed, names from popular music have dominated the English music scene over the last forty years. It is interesting that although the Beatles had their first number one hit in 1963, a CD of their songs was again at the top of the charts for a long period in 1999. It is rather unlikely that our Australian or Icelander would give the name of one of England's classical composers or jazz musicians, simply because England is not well known for such music. In the eyes of the world, England means pop!

Beginnings

Of course English music did not start with The Beatles, though it may seem like that to many young people. In England, as elsewhere, the origins of national music lie in the songs sung and dance music played by ordinary country people (folk music in a real sense). This music passed from village to village, and was handed down – with slight changes made, but still in an unwritten form – from generation to generation. Troubadors or minstrels (travelling writers and performers of songs) played a vital part in spreading songs and dances from town to town, and even from country to country. The English song 'Summer is icumen in' dates from the thirteenth century and is still much loved and regularly performed today. It is not a simple piece, however, but has a complex six-part harmonic structure.

The popularity of folk song as a means of entertainment declined with the gradual improvement of transport and the movement of agricultural workers to the cities, especially during the Industrial Revolution in the nineteenth century. Fortunately, England has been able to preserve hundreds of its old songs and tunes thanks to the efforts of two men: **Cecil Sharp** (1859–1924) and **Ralph Vaughan Williams** (1872–1958). Both were collectors of such music, but Vaughan Williams (see page 90) was also a composer who used folk songs in his work, and was known too for his symphonies, ballet and film music.

Modern 'folk music' is very different from what Sharp and Vaughan Williams had in mind: they would not recognize the instruments (sometimes electric), the sound and the setting in which the music is played. However, they would probably approve of the fact that those bands and singers who have made their names as 'folk singers' usually compose their own songs and frequently sing or adapt those which the two men themselves had originally collected.

Music in church and court

In the Middle Ages, choral music was the most popular form, much of it produced for use in church. England had a great reputation in this field, particularly in unaccompanied choral works or music for keyboard instruments such as the organ, harpsichord, lute or clavichord.The first English composer to have an international reputation was **John Dunstable** (1390–1453) who is known to have influenced his European contemporaries, especially in the use of counterpoint (the mixing of two different melodies in the same piece of music).

Patronage

Kings and queens in those days were very fond of music. They not only had their own musicians in the court, but also requested new works by selected composers, and arranged special performances for their own pleasure and that of their visitors. Certain kings even composed music themselves: **Henry VIII**, who wrote several masses, anthems and songs, is the best-known. Many great English composers of the sixteenth and seventeenth centuries owed their living to the patronage of the monarch. Three such were **John Dowland** (1562–1626), **Thomas Campion** (1567–1620), and **Orlando Gibbons** (1583–1625). Each in his time was a member or 'gentleman' of The Chapel Royal (providing music for church and state occasions), as were the following, more celebrated composers:

- **Thomas Tallis** (1505–1585) was a master of counterpoint, his most famous piece being the beautiful *Spem in Alium*, a motet (sacred music for unaccompanied singers) for forty voices – a remarkable technical achievement.

- **William Byrd** (1543–1623) was one of the founders of the English madrigal movement (this form of song for three to six unaccompanied voices originated in Italy). He also wrote three beautiful masses which use counterpoint very effectively.

- In 1601, Byrd's contemporary **Thomas Morley** (1577–1603) edited *The Triumphs of Oriana*, a collection of 29 madrigals by different composers, written in honour of Queen Elizabeth I. Morley was also a friend of William Shakespeare, for whose play *As You Like It* he composed the famous song 'It was a lover and his lass'.

Purcell

Henry Purcell

Perhaps the first great name of English music is Henry Purcell (1659-1695). Despite his short life, the list of his musical achievements is long. He was an organist at Westminster Abbey, wrote music for the theatre, for King Charles II, and for the coronations of both James II and William III. He is perhaps best-known today for his songs, his church music, 'semi-operas' and instrumental music (described in later centuries as in the 'baroque' style, meaning rather grand, complex compositions). The formation of The Purcell Society in 1876 helped re-establish his reputation and promote his works; twentieth-century composers such as Vaughan-Williams, Holst and Britten also acknowledged their debt to him. If you wish to listen to some Purcell, try his *Fantasias for Strings*, his harpsichord suites, or his choral works such as *Ode for St Cecilia's Day* or *Come Ye Sons of Art*.

Handel

During Purcell's lifetime, opera began to be popular in England, but it was not until George Frideric Handel (1685–1759) arrived in England that this musical genre reached new heights. Although Handel was born in Germany, England can claim him as a countryman since he came here in 1714, when his patron from Hanover became King George I, and was naturalized as an Englishman in 1726. Every music-lover probably associates Handel with works which have become immensely popular over the years, and feature regularly in concert or choir performances: his oratorio *The Messiah* (which includes 'The Hallelujah Chorus'), *The Water Music*, *Music for the Royal Fireworks*, and *Zadok the Priest* (which was written for George II's coronation in 1727 and has been sung at the coronation of every English monarch since then). Handel's most original contribution to the art of music is said to be his development of the genre of dramatic oratorios, such as in *Esther* or *Acis and Galatea*. Beethoven spoke of him thus: 'go and learn of him how to achieve great effects with simple means'; while Haydn, with tears in his eyes, is said to have risen to his feet after hearing *The Hallelujah Chorus* in Westminster Abbey and proclaimed, 'He is the master of us all!'

Four popular composers

Gay and Arne

It is often written that the popularity of Handel's music dominated English music for 150 years after his death. Certainly, this was a low period with no other great names in classical music until we come to Elgar at the end of the nineteenth century. However, it is worth mentioning four composers who have left their mark in different ways: one is **John Gay** (1685–1732) who wrote the dialogue and lyrics of *The Beggar's Opera* in 1728, while his colleague, **John Pepusch**, chose and arranged the music, using popular tunes of the day. This was a parody of fashionable Italian-style operas (such as those written by Handel) – it was set in a prison and featured criminals and prostitutes as characters. The opera was new in many ways and showed aspects of life never before represented on stage. It has remained popular, was much imitated in Europe, and is regularly performed today.

Thomas Arne (1710–1778) composed the work which is broadcast all over the world each September when the Last Night of the Proms (see Chapter Six) takes place: 'Rule, Britannia'. In fact it comes from a masque he wrote entitled *Alfred*. The music still used today for many of the songs in Shakespeare's plays was also composed by Arne.

'G and S'

Far greater than Gay and Arne in terms of worldwide popularity are 'G and S', as they are commonly known: Sir W S Gilbert (1836–1911) and Sir Arthur Sullivan (1842–1900). They wrote 14 comic operas (or operettas) between 1871 and 1896, most of which were performed at the Savoy Theatre in London, and which therefore became known as 'The Savoy Operas'. The best-known works are *Trial by Jury*, *HMS Pinafore*, *The Pirates of Penzance*, *Iolanthe*, *The Yeomen of the Guard*, *The Mikado* and *The Gondoliers*. These are widely performed around the English-speaking world today, by both professional and amateur companies.

Why are they so popular? The operas are a successful blend of Gilbert's satirical and witty verses, and Sullivan's inventive and catchy melodies. It seems to make no difference to audiences that the subjects of the satire (often aspects of British life in the nineteenth century such as the legal system, women's education, the navy) no longer have as much relevance today. The happy combination of music and lyrics is what appeals. In fact, Sullivan, who had won a Mendelssohn scholarship at the age of 14 enabling him to study in Germany, and later became a Professor of Music, wished to be taken seriously as a classical musician; yet his 'serious' works were seen as heavy and uninspired, and are rarely played today. Fortunately, his successful collaboration with Gilbert has given English music something unique in the field of popular entertainment.

Elgar

'I've got a tune that will knock 'em flat! ... a tune like that comes once in a lifetime'. These are the words (quoted in Scholes, 1970) of Edward Elgar (1857–1934), talking about the 'tune' that has ensured his name is known around the world. It is the trio section of one of his *Pomp and Circumstance Marches*. King Edward VII suggested that it be given words: thus it became known in 1902 as 'Land of Hope and Glory', and is still one of the pieces played and sung every year at the Last Night of the Proms, as a kind of unofficial national anthem. Elgar is perhaps the only great classical musician that England can lay claim to in the Victorian age, yet he had a long struggle to establish himself as a composer. It was the Three Choirs festival (see Chapter Six) which gave him his opportunity. He lived near Worcester and began to conduct and write works for festival performances there. His best-loved compositions are *Variations on an Original Theme* (otherwise known as *The Enigma Variations*), *Sea Pictures* (a song cycle), *The Dream of Gerontius* (a religious work based on Cardinal Henry Newman's poem), *The Cockaigne Overture*, and his violin and cello concertos. Elgar was perhaps the first great composer to appreciate the importance of the gramophone, and in his later years he made many recordings of his music. Elgar's work is always said to be very English in style and effect, yet it was also greatly appreciated in Germany – a real mark of success for English music – until the First World War began.

Classical music of the twentieth century

Of those English classical composers whose music was mainly composed in the last century, there is perhaps only one name which can rank with the greatest, and that is **Benjamin Britten** (1913–1976). Britten composed a wide range of music: choral works, solo songs, music for documentary films, operas. The latter are chiefly responsible for his reputation and include *Peter Grimes, The Rape of Lucretia, Albert Herring, Billy Budd, The Turn of the Screw, A Midsummer Night's Dream,* and *Death in Venice.* The list shows that, like most writers of opera, Britten often found his initial inspiration in literature. Much of his work deals with serious contemporary themes such as the causes of evil, isolation, and intolerance. Classical music is also indebted to him for having established the Aldeburgh Festival (see Chapter Six).

Behind Britten in terms of reputation, but still popular today, come composers such as **Gustav Holst** (1874–1934) and **Ralph Vaughan Williams** (1872–1958). They were contemporaries and friends, both born in Gloucestershire and both interested in adapting traditional folk music for their compositions. Holst (who had a Swedish forefather, hence his name) was chiefly known for *The Planets*, a seven-movement orchestral piece designed to represent the human temperaments that astrology associates with each planet. The theme from the Jupiter movement was subsequently adapted for the much-loved song, 'I vow to thee my country' (and was chosen by Princess Diana as one of the pieces played at her wedding).

Vaughan Williams was very versatile, writing music in almost every genre, including concertos for neglected instruments such as the tuba and harmonica. He was also one of many twentieth-century composers to write film music, his best-known work in this genre being the score for *Scott of the Antarctic* in 1948. Perhaps because of his use of folk tunes, Vaughan Williams' best work is always thought to be specially English, suggesting the peace and beauty of the English countryside. His most performed and recorded works include *Fantasia on a Theme of Thomas Tallis*, his opera *Sir John in Love* (about Shakespeare's character Sir John Falstaff), his *Pastoral Symphony*, his *Fifth Symphony,* and *The Lark Ascending* (a piece for violin and orchestra).

Another composer who worked in the cinema was **William Walton** (1902–1983). His celebrated scores include Laurence Olivier's great films of Shakespeare's plays *Henry V* and *Hamlet*. Most of Walton's greatest successes came early on: at the age of 20 he wrote the accompanying music (including some jazz) for *Facade*, a kind of avant garde satirical entertainment in which the writer Edith Sitwell recited some of her poems through a megaphone! Then at 29 he wrote *Belshazzar's Feast*, a work for chorus and orchestra, based on the Bible story.

After Britten's death, **Michael Tippett** (1905–1998) was considered England's leading composer. He was a man of strong principles and, as a conscientious objector (a pacifist opposed to war), was imprisoned during the Second World War. Tippett is best known for his oratorio, *A Child of our Time*, and his operas, *The Midsummer Marriage* and *The Knot Garden*.

England can boast no major female composers. However, mention must be made of **Dame Ethel Smyth** (1858–1944) who was equally famous as an active feminist. She demonstrated on behalf of the Suffragettes (campaigners for women's rights), and in 1911 was even put in prison for a few months. Here she composed the Suffragettes' battle-song, 'The March of Women', and conducted her fellow-prisoners singing it, using a toothbrush to beat time!

Contemporary classical music

Composers

Although it is impossible to know which of today's classical composers will still be admired in the next century, here are a few whose works are likely to stand the test of time.

		Best-known works
Alexander Goehr	b. 1932	*Arden must die* (opera), *Death of Moses* (oratorio), *Sing, Ariel* (cantata)
Harrison Birtwistle	b. 1934	*Mask of Orpheus* and *Gawain* (operas)

Peter Maxwell Davies	b. 1934	*Taverner, The Lighthouse* (operas)
John Tavener	b. 1944	*Song for Athene, The Whale* (opera), *The Protecting Veil* (for cello and strings)
Michael Nyman	b. 1944	Film music (e.g. *The Piano), The Man who mistook his Wife for a Hat* (chamber opera)
Oliver Knussen	b. 1952	*Where the Wild Things are* (opera), *Whitman Settings* (for soprano and orchestra)
Mark-Anthony Turnage	b. 1960	*Greek* (opera), *Your Rockaby* (saxophone concerto)

Orchestras

England has numerous orchestras of high quality. The 'big five' (in terms of reputation, size and number of recordings) are the LPO (London Philharmonic Orchestra), the LSO (London Symphony Orchestra, which, founded in 1904, is the oldest of the five), the RPO (Royal Philharmonic Orchestra), The Philharmonia, and the BBC Symphony Orchestra. Yet there are plenty of others of varying sizes, both in London and the regions: for example, the Academy of Ancient Music, the London Sinfonietta, the English Chamber Orchestra, the Academy of St Martin-in-the Fields (which performs in a famous London church), the London Mozart Players, the CBSO (City of Birmingham Symphony Orchestra), the Hallé Orchestra (based in Manchester), the Northern Sinfonia (Newcastle), the Bournemouth Symphony Orchestra and the National Youth Orchestra.

Amateur music

All over England there are amateur groups, from operatic societies to pub bands, who spend part of their free time making music. Brass band music is still common in many Northern towns. This kind of music (where only brass instruments are used) is linked with the rise of industry in that part of England in the late nineteenth century. The successful film, *Brassed Off*, made in 1996, depicts very well the appeal and competitive spirit of such bands. Elsewhere, other kinds of music-making flourish, for example, community choirs, string quartets or small orchestras. Such groups may give annual performances in local halls or schools, or just enjoy making private music for its own sake. Indeed, many of England's best composers and musicians began their careers in such a way.

Conductors and performers

Though England may not be as rich in world-class performers as the United States or perhaps some European countries, it nevertheless has a considerable number of performers and conductors whose names are very well known in the classical field.

Conductors		Achievements
Henry Wood	1869–1944	First conductor of the London 'Proms'
Thomas Beecham	1879–1961	Conductor and wit; established the Royal Philharmonic Orchestra
Adrian Boult	1889–1983	Chief conductor of the BBC Symphony Orchestra and later of the London Philharmonic
Malcolm Sargent	1895–1967	Chief conductor of The Proms from 1957
John Barbirolli	1899–1970	Conductor of the Hallé Orchestra, Manchester, 1943–1970
Georg Solti	1912–1997	Music director of The Royal Opera House; later, principal conductor of the London Philharmonic
Neville Marriner	b. 1924	Conductor who established the Academy of St Martin-in-the-Fields
Colin Davis	b. 1927	Chief conductor, Royal Opera House and later of the London Symphony Orchestra

John Eliot Gardiner	b. 1943	Conductor of early music performances. Founder of the Monteverdi Orchestra.
Simon Rattle	b.1955	For nearly twenty years Chief Conductor of the City of Birmingham Symphony Orchestra
Performers		**Achievements**
Kathleen Ferrier	1912–1953	Contralto, famous for her work in opera, oratorio and folk song
Yehudi Menuhin	1916–1999	Violinist, and founder of a school for children with special musical ability
Dennis Brain	1921–1957	Horn player. Best known for his recordings of Mozart works
Janet Baker	b. 1933	Soprano famous for her performances of baroque music and English operas
John Ogdon	1937–1989	Pianist and composer, famous for playing contemporary work
John Lill	b. 1944	Pianist, well known for his concerts of Beethoven and Liszt's work
Jacqueline du Pré	1945-1987	Cellist, famous especially for her performances of Elgar
Nigel Kennedy	b. 1956	Violinist, now known as just 'Kennedy'. Plays in many styles. Best known for recordings of Elgar and Vivaldi

Musicals

One name which could equally well be mentioned in a chapter on literature is that of a man whose talents included theatre, cinema, song-writing and performing, and whose wit is legendary:

Noël Coward (1899–1973). The brilliant songs he wrote and
performed in his prime (the 1930s and 1940s) – both romantic and
comic – are still popular today: 'Poor little rich girl', 'A Room with
a View', 'Mad about the Boy', 'Don't put your daughter on the
stage, Mrs Worthington', and 'Mad Dogs and Englishmen'.

Coward was as famous for his plays (such as *Private Lives, Blithe
Spirit, Design for Living* and *Hay Fever*), as for his work in the
cinema, in particular the excellent war film, *In Which We Serve,*
and his script for the classic British weepie, *Brief Encounter.* It was
Coward who expressed so well the whole basis of popular music in
a line in one of his plays: 'extraordinary how potent cheap music
is', meaning that simple tunes and lyrics can still move and affect
us however many times we hear them.

England's other distinguished writers of popular musicals in the
twentieth century include **Lionel Bart** (1930–1999) who wrote
shows with a truly Cockney (from the East End of London)
character and humour. His most famous musical was *Oliver!*
(1960), which was adapted from Charles Dickens' novel, *Oliver
Twist.* So popular was the musical, with its many excellent songs,
that it was soon made into a film, winning several Oscars,
including Best Picture, in 1968. Bart's two other best musicals
were *Fings ain't what they used to be* (1959) about the changes in
the lives of Londoners since the Second World War, and *Blitz*
(1962) which was set during that war.

More recently, **Andrew Lloyd-Webber** (b. 1948) has had a
constant stream of hit musicals in the West End (London's theatre
centre). His first success at the age of 20, with Tim Rice as his
lyricist, was the 'rock opera' *Joseph and the Technicolour
Dreamcoat* in 1968, followed by another with a Biblical theme,
Jesus Christ Superstar, in 1971. Lloyd-Webber followed this with
other huge international hits including *Evita* (1976), *Cats* (1981),
Starlight Express (1984), *Phantom of the Opera* (1986), *Sunset
Boulevard* (1993) and *The Beautiful Game (*2000). His work seems
to divide opinion: a large section of the public love his musicals for
their strong melodies and dramatic staging, while the critics
generally describe them as dull and musically undistinguished.

Folk song

As was mentioned above, the study of folk music was revived in the late nineteenth century, and began to influence the work of classical composers. However, in terms of folk music for the mass market, interest only followed – as often happens – where the United States led. The revival in this genre across the Atlantic, notably with **Pete Seeger**, **Bob Dylan** and **Joan Baez**, made it easier for new British groups with an interest in traditional folk music – but often with a rock beat – to make an impact in the 1960s and 1970s. **Pentangle**, **The Incredible String Band**, **Fairport Convention**, **The Albion Band** and **Steeleye Span** were perhaps the most successful. Among the best individual performers still working today are the singer/guitarist/composers **Martin Carthy** (b. 1940) and **Ralph McTell** (b. 1944), and the former's wife, **Norma Waterson** (b. 1939): all have made memorable records, both in the traditional and modern folk styles. (See the 'Taking it further' section at the end of the chapter for suggestions of the best of English folk.)

Jazz

Although there is quite a large audience for jazz on record and on radio (there is a commercial radio station, Jazz FM, in London), England does not have a strong reputation for creating jazz. However, three jazz performers stand out.

Johnny Dankworth (b. 1927) is a composer, bandleader and saxophonist, who has done much to pioneer modern jazz in Britain. Not only has he composed many excellent film scores (eg for *Saturday Night and Sunday Morning* and *The Servant*), and composed jazz suites based on the works of Dickens and Shakespeare, but he has also – together with his wife, the jazz singer, **Cleo Laine** (b. 1927) – set up a small arts centre in which promising new musicians can receive training and give concerts.

Ronnie Scott (1927–1996) is less famous for performing than for the fact that in 1959 he opened a famous jazz club in London. The club is now in Frith Street in Soho and still bears Ronnie Scott's name. It is the best venue in London at which to hear good jazz, often played by international stars.

Courtney Pine (b. 1964) is the leading young jazz performer in England today. He is a saxophonist whose work shows many influences, including soul, reggae and Asian sounds.

Pop and rock

If there is anything for which England is world famous, apart from Shakespeare, the Royal Family, and drinking tea, it must be its pop and rock music. The group which did most to establish this fame is, of course, The Beatles. Their arrival was perfectly timed for maximum success: in the 1950s Britain had become richer, there was almost full employment, and the post-war 'baby boom' generation had become teenagers and was ready to spend its money on entertainment, clothes and music. The popular singers of the 1940s and early 1950s had been crooners in the romantic style of Frank Sinatra. Then rock and roll hit the world of music with a huge impact. The influence of American stars such as Elvis Presley, Bill Haley, Little Richard and Chuck Berry was felt in Britain which produced its own rock and roll stars, including Cliff Richard.

Cliff Richard

Cliff Richard (born Harry Webb in 1940) spent the first eight years of his life in India. His first number one hit (the 'Top 20' idea having been introduced to Britain only in 1955) was 'Living Doll' in 1959. He has been remarkably successful since then in maintaining his popularity despite changing public tastes. He began starring in a short series of unmemorable musical films in 1959, and has continued to have hit records into the 1990s – a tribute to his youthful good looks, pleasant voice and ability to adapt his style to appeal to both old and new audiences. Richard's strong Christian beliefs have led him to do a lot of charity work. He was awarded a knighthood in 1995.

The rise of the regions

In the late 1950s, the huge popularity of rock and roll led to the opening of more clubs and dance halls, and the creation of hundreds of groups, usually formed of a drummer, a bass guitarist and two rhythm guitarists, with one or another of these players as the vocalist (singer). Acoustic instruments were now set aside in favour of electrification and amplification. This was the background against which the 'Liverpool Sound' or the 'Mersey Beat' (the Mersey being the river in Liverpool) became famous. The late 1950s had also seen the rise of the working-class regional hero in novels, plays and the cinema, and now music followed. Many of the new pop heroes of the 1960s came from such backgrounds: **The Beatles**, **Gerry and the Pacemakers**, and **The Searchers** from Liverpool; **The Animals** from Newcastle; **The Moody Blues** from Birmingham; **Herman's Hermits** and **Freddie and the Dreamers** both from Manchester. It was now not only London which set the style for the rest of the nation to follow.

The Beatles

John Lennon (1940–1980), Paul McCartney (b. 1942), George Harrison (1943–2001) and Ringo Starr (b. 1940) were four talented boys from ordinary backgrounds. Their early music was a mix of their favourite styles, American rhythm and blues and rock and roll, but they developed their own distinctive sound. A lot of their early success was due to the influence of their manager, Brian Epstein, and to their musical arranger, George Martin. Their first number one hit, 'From me to You', arrived in 1963, and Beatlemania followed. There was an extraordinary worldwide interest in the group, or the 'Fab Four', as they soon became known in the media. They were mobbed by crowds at each public appearance, their

The Beatles

every public statement was reported and analyzed, their clothes and hairstyles were widely imitated, and their records sold in millions. Luckily they had genuine charm, wit and talent, and parents warmed to them. Two well-received films followed: *A Hard Day's Night* (1964) and *Help!* (1965).

The Beatles stopped touring in 1966 and their music now entered a new phase. Lennon and McCartney's skill as composers was already apparent from their earlier albums, *Rubber Soul* and *Revolver*. However, it was perhaps the appearance of *Sergeant Pepper's Lonely Hearts Club Band* in 1967 that made critics and music fans of all tastes aware that here was something special in pop music, both innovative and memorable. This record perhaps marked the point when pop music began to be taken seriously in England by those who had previously ignored it. The songs in the album, all skilfully arranged by George Martin, revealed the full range of the Beatles' talents, from 'She's Leaving Home' and 'A Day in the Life' to 'When I'm 64' and 'Lovely Rita Meter Maid'. Their three final albums before the group split up in 1970, *The Beatles* (also known as The White Album), *Abbey Road* and *Let it Be*, confirmed this high reputation and contained some more of their finest songs: 'Back in the USSR', 'Julia', 'Here comes the Sun', 'Something', and 'Because'.

The Beatles' success continues even thirty years after they broke up and went their separate ways, each going on to record individual albums. As mentioned at the start of this chapter, the collection of the Beatles' number one hits, entitled *The Beatles 1*, released in November 1999, sold nearly 10 million copies and was number one in the album charts on both sides of the Atlantic for several weeks. The Beatles have conquered a new generation of fans.

The Rolling Stones

The only English group that can be said to come at all close to the Beatles' success in terms of long-lasting fame and reputation is The Rolling Stones. Though they are all now in their mid to late fifties, the Stones are still touring. In fact right from the start of their career they were famed – more so than the Beatles – for the power and excitement of their live concerts. They too in their early years were heavily influenced by American music, especially rhythm and blues, and many of their first records (eg 'Not Fade Away', 'It's All Over Now', and 'Time is on My Side') were versions of American artists' songs. By the mid-1960s they had found their own style and began to write good songs of their own, *Satisfaction, Paint it Black* and *Get off My Cloud,* being three successful examples. Their best-selling albums all came in the late 1960s and early 1970s (*Aftermath, Between the Buttons, Beggars Banquet*, and *Exile on Main Street*) and since then they have never quite been able to recapture the creative spirit and the special rock and blues mix which typified their style at its best.

The Stones were always seen as a more 'dangerous', rebellious and sexier group than The Beatles. From the start they wore stranger clothes and had longer hair – and were less popular with parents. Mick Jagger, with his powerful vocal style and energetic dancing, and Keith Richard, with his dark brooding looks and distinctive rhythm guitar solos, were the key performers and writers. Together they wrote some memorable songs, one of which expresses the great truth: 'I know, it's only rock 'n' roll, but I like it'.

Other groups from the 1960s

Apart from these giants, which other groups deserve to be remembered for their work in that musically rich era? Of those who made their names in the 1960s, the popularity of the following live on today, even though most are no longer working as groups:

Groups	Lead singers	Best songs / albums
The Who	Roger Daltrey	*My Generation* (song), *Tommy* and *Quadrophenia* (rock operas)
The Animals	Eric Burdon	*House of the Rising Sun, We Gotta get out of this Place* (songs)
The Kinks	Ray Davies (singer/writer)	*You Really Got Me, Sunny Afternoon, Waterloo Sunset, Dead End Street* (songs)
The Moody Blues	Justin Hayward	*Nights in White Satin* (song), *Days of Future Passed* (album)
Procul Harum	Gary Brooker	*A Whiter Shade of Pale* (song), *A Salty Dog* (album)
Manfred Mann	Paul Jones	*54321, Do Wah Diddy Diddy, Pretty Flamingo* (songs)

Dusty Springfield

Though all-women pop groups were unknown in Britain in the 1960s, there was one woman singer who achieved critical success and large record sales in both Britain and America.

Dusty Springfield (1939–1999) was a white singer with the voice and style of a black soul or rhythm and blues artist. She sang as part of a group at first, but went solo in 1963, and had a series of hit records, for example, 'I only want to be with you', 'Wishin' and Hopin'', 'You don't have to say you love me', and 'Son of a Preacher Man'. Her career declined in the 1970s but at her peak her strong, versatile voice and attractive personality made her a favourite with a wide range of audiences.

Six solo rock stars

The careers of the following six male singers began in the 1960s, 1970s or 1980s; their music is still hugely popular throughout the world.

Elton John

(Sir) Elton John, (another pop knight, like Cliff Richard and Paul McCartney), was born in 1947, with the name of Reginald Dwight. He took his new name in 1967 when playing with singer Long John Baldry and saxophone player, Elton Dean. In 1968, Elton met the lyricist, Bernie Taupin, who has written some of his best and most popular songs. In 1970, he toured America for the first time. Then, as now, his extravagant stage personality and mixture of rock and roll piano with soulful singing made him a big success. His best albums are perhaps *Honky Chateau*, *Goodbye Yellow Brick Road* (which contained his great hit, 'Candle in the Wind'), *Too Low for Zero*, and *Ice on Fire*. In 1979, Elton was the first Western pop star to perform in Russia. Another distinction was his memorable performance of a specially rewritten 'Candle in the Wind' at his friend Princess Diana's funeral at Westminster Abbey in 1997.

David Bowie

David Bowie (b. 1947) was born David Jones. To avoid confusion with another pop singer with the same name, in 1966 he switched his surname to Bowie – after the American hunting knife. David

Bowie's background is more interesting than that of most pop stars: early in his career he took saxophone lessons, studied Buddhism, learned the skill of mime and worked as a dancer. These experiences certainly had their effect on Bowie's musical style and stage performance. His first hit was the song, 'Space Oddity'. In his 1972 song collection, *The Rise and Fall of Ziggy Stardust and the Spiders from Mars*, he performed the role of an alien from space who becomes a huge rock star. His strange costumes and powerful stage presence made him a star worldwide, and had a big influence on the rise of punk and glam rock (see page 104). Bowie's work since then has been through many changes of style, and has continued to be varied and experimental, including rock, soul, cool fifties crooner-style, music videos, films, modern dance, internet singles, film music, digital CDs, etc. Perhaps his best albums since the early 1970s have been *Young Americans*, *Let's Dance* and *Black Tie, White Noise*.

Rod Stewart

Born in London in 1945, Stewart spent several years working with various groups, notably The Faces, before he went solo and had his first big hit with 'Maggie May'. His throaty, sexy voice and energetic stage act gave him great success all over the world, and his versatility enabled him to have hits with both slow ballads and rock and roll records. His best albums are perhaps those from the 1970s: *Gasoline Alley, Every Picture Tells a Story, Atlantic Crossing* and *A Night on the Town*. Though Stewart has lived in California since the 1970s, he still tours regularly and has Top 20 hits, mainly now with slower ballads.

Freddie Mercury

Mercury (1946–1991) was known for his tremendous stage performances with his group Queen (especially in big sports stadia), and for his powerful voice, suited to both rock and romantic ballads. Queen's anthem-like hits 'Bohemian Rhapsody', 'We Will Rock You' and 'We are the Champions' have become pop classics. Sadly, Mercury also achieved fame as the first rock star to die of the AIDS illness. Queen's best work can be found in the albums *A Night at the Opera, News of the World, The Works* and *The Miracle*.

Sting

Sting (born Gordon Sumner in 1951) has become one of England's most creative – and most political – singer/song-writers, and has built a high reputation worldwide. He has often given concerts for Amnesty International (the organization which helps those who it believes have been unfairly imprisoned), and has written many songs making social, political or environmental comments. His best work with his group, The Police, was the album *Regatta de Blanc.* Since 1984, his albums as a solo artist include *Synchronicity, The Dream of the Blue Turtles,* and *Brand New Day.*

George Michael

George Michael is another handsome face who achieved great fame in the 1980s and is today a worldwide star. Born Georgios Panayiotou in 1963 in London, he first found success with the disco duo Wham! in the early 1980s. In 1986 he went solo and his first album, *Faith*, produced six hit singles in the United States. He developed into a strong 'white soul' singer, able to succeed with both big ballads and the faster dance music with which he had first attracted attention.

England leads the way...

Over the last thirty or so years English pop music has led the world in its range and quality, starting several new trends. Some of the main ones are described below:

Progressive rock

Progressive rock bands began their careers in the late 1960s or early 1970s and specialized in spectacular stage shows, often based on a central theme, combining heavy rock music with a wide range of other musical styles. This was a distinctively English development, which was soon adopted by American rock groups. Certainly, the psychedelic (affecting the mind) drugs popular at the time were said to have played a part in the creation of the surreal and often obscure lyrics which sometimes accompanied the music. This was written mainly to be listened – not danced – to, and so it generally avoided a continuous rock beat. The Beatles had an influence on these groups, particularly in their willingness to use other types of music (Indian, jazz, baroque, etc) in their compositions.

Progressive rock bands

Groups which performed in this style, in addition to Procul Harum and The Moody Blues already mentioned above, included:

Band	Leader / lead singer	Best songs / albums
Jethro Tull	Ian Anderson	*Living in the Past* (song), *Thick as a Brick* (album)
Emerson, Lake and Palmer	Keith Emerson	*Pictures at an Exhibition* (album)
Pink Floyd	Syd Barrett, David Gilmour	*Dark Side of the Moon*, *A Saucerful of Secrets* (albums)
Yes	Jon Anderson, Rick Wakeman	*The Yes Album, Close to the Edge* (albums)
Electric Light Orchestra	Jeff Lynne	*Eldorado, A New World Record* (albums)
Genesis	Peter Gabriel, Phil Collins	*Foxtrot, Selling England by the Pound* (albums)

Punk

The punk movement of the 1970s began in England, and was then taken up in other countries. It was partly a reaction against progressive rock's thoughtful, hippie-style music and imagery. The punk bands (**The Sex Pistols, The Clash, The Stranglers, The Damned**, to name some of the chief ones) were, as their names suggest, out to shock – through their hairstyles, clothes, and attitudes, just as much as through their music. Theirs was a loud, urgent, angry sound, with lyrics which often carried a mocking, anti-government (or anti-everything!) message:

> *God save the Queen,*
> *She ain't no human being,*
> *There is no future in England's dreaming.*

> (From 'God Save the Queen' by The Sex Pistols, 1977)

The groups' success relied largely on stage shows, where their aggressive behaviour (swearing, spitting, throwing things) created an extra impact, rather than on recordings, where a certain lack of musical skill revealed itself. The typical flavour of punk can be heard on The Sex Pistols' album, *Anarchy in the UK* (1976*)*, and seen in the film *The Great Rock'n' Roll Swindle*, made about them in 1980.

Punks

Glam rock

Glam rock was also a reaction against the seriousness of progressive rock. Here the main figures (**David Bowie**, **Elton John**, **Gary Glitter**, **Marc Bolan**, **Roxy Music**, and **Queen**) wanted to emphasize the 'glamorous' aspect of their appearance as much as their music. Great attention was paid to the style and originality of their hair, clothes and make-up, often suggesting bi-sexuality. Apart from Bowie and John, two other key figures to emerge from this movement were **Bryan Ferry** of Roxy Music and, as mentioned above, Freddie Mercury of Queen. In the mid-1970s, Ferry went on to a solo career, where, with his distinctive style of singing, he was able to indulge his taste for sad, romantic ballads. Key albums are *Roxy Music, Manifesto* and *Avalon*.

Heavy metal

Heavy metal, like punk, started in the 1970s and was mainly popular with a working-class, predominantly male, public. It was louder, faster and more aggressive than traditional rock and roll, and featured skilful solo guitar, fierce drumming and high-pitched vocals, with no 'message' other than sheer enjoyment of the sound. Typical bands in this style were **Status Quo**, **Led Zeppelin**, **Black Sabbath**, **Def Leppard** and **Deep Purple**; the regular themes of their songs were sex, drugs, the occult (or magical powers) and rock 'n' roll itself. Key albums from this phase are Led Zeppelin's *Physical Graffiti*, Def Leppard's *Hysteria*, Black Sabbath's *Heaven and Hell*, and Deep Purple's *Deep Purple in Rock*.

Reggae, ethnic music and politics

Reggae became popular in England in the 1970s among young people of Caribbean origin. The appeal of its catchy rhythm and its cultural associations soon attracted English pop groups, as did many other types of ethnic music. Even though North America remains a major influence, the music of the Caribbean, India, Africa and South America, have had a considerable impact on the style and sound of British popular music. The punk band, **The Clash**, and other groups of that era – **The Police** (with Sting), **UB-40** and **Madness** – were attracted to reggae, as well as to ska (which is reggae with a faster beat).

The 1970s was a period of high unemployment and strikes in England. String was not the only singer to express political views in songs written at this time. Several of the 'new wave' groups – **The Jam** (led by Paul Weller), **Elvis Costello**, and **Dire Straits** (Mark Knopfler) – made strong statements in their work.

The New Romantics

This is another movement to which English groups of the late 1970s and early 1980s belonged. Both disco and electronic music (in particular the synthesizer) began to establish themselves at this time, and groups such as **Spandau Ballet**, **Ultravox**, **Duran Duran**, **Culture Club** and **Depeche Mode** made use of both styles in their music. The romantic element in their music – attractive, well-written love songs, accompanied by a strong electronic beat – was also a reaction against the harsh edges of punk. It is interesting to note that Martin Kemp, a member of Spandau Ballet, who, like other good-looking pop stars (for example, David Bowie and Sting), eventually tried acting, could, until recently, be seen playing one of the main characters in the popular BBC soap, *Eastenders*.

House, Jungle, Techno, and Garage

These styles of music have been popular with young people in England over the last few years. What kinds of music are they?

- **House**: a blend of disco, soul and synthesizer music, mixed using computer programs, the whole being a hard, loud, simple sound, well suited to wild energetic dancing in clubs or at raves (which could attract over twenty thousand people each weekend). Although House music originated in the United States, it was English DJs and producers who made it popular with a wide audience.

- **Jungle**: another type of popular dance music, which developed in the 1990s. It is also based on a strong electronic beat, with a heavy drum and bass element. The soulful lyrics used often focus on the pleasures and problems of city life. The albums, *Timeless* by the DJ Goldie, and *New Forms* by DJ/producer, Roni Size, are good examples, the latter winning the respected Mercury Music Prize in 1997.

- **Techno**: a fast, very loud, technologically-produced sound, which also mixes in samples to produce a strong, repetitive dance rhythm. Chief makers of such music are acts like **Leftfield**, **Orbital**, and **The Chemical Brothers**, who appear both at festivals and in clubs either as performers of their own music or as remixers of other bands' work.

- **UK Garage**: another type of powerful drum-and-bass style dance-club music. Although it originated in black American gospel and soul music, it has been given new life by English DJs and producers, such as the So Solid Crew, who have added English sounds of rave and hardcore to make UK Garage into something quite new and commercially successful .

Britpop

This was the general name given in the 1990s to a new wave of successful English bands who made a big impact in the United States and Europe, as well as on home soil. The most successful have been:

- **Oasis**: led by the argumentative Gallagher brothers from Manchester. They have presented a rough, working-class image, but their music has had wide appeal. *Definitely Maybe*, *(What's the Story), Morning Glory?*, and *Be Here Now* have been their most successful albums so far.

- **Blur**: with Damon Albarn as their lead singer, Blur have produced several interesting albums, containing many well-written songs, which are sometimes rather sad and cynical in tone. Their best work so far is on *Parklife*.

- **Pulp**: this band started in the late 1970s, but only achieved wide success with their albums *His and Hers* and *Different Class* in the 1990s. The lead singer, Jarvis Cocker, has shown himself to be a clever writer too. His songs tend to deal in a humorous way with the bleak realities of urban life.

- **Massive Attack**: come from Bristol (also the source of other popular 1990s bands, **Portishead** and **Tricky**) and became one of the biggest dance groups of the 1990s, with their lively mix of reggae and American-based influences. Their albums, *Blue Lines* and *No Protection,* achieved great critical and popular success.

- **Radiohead**: have become a 'super-group' mainly on the basis of the huge success which greeted their album *OK Computer* in 1997. Two years earlier they had had modest success with *The Bends*. Their thoughtful songs, mainly written and sung by Thom Yorke, offer a distinctive and poetic blend of soulful rock.

- **The Spice Girls**: it is perhaps sad to end this list of the best of English pop and rock music with a group which lacks any special talent or musical distinction. However, The Spice Girls must be mentioned, simply because they are, in their way, a phenomenon. Their first disc, 'Wannabe', in 1996 was an instant number one hit, as was their first album, *Spice*. After a long world tour, they achieved similar success in the United States, Asia and Europe. Their second album, *Spiceworld*, was an even bigger hit; it was followed with a film, *Spiceworld the Movie*. Since then, one Spice Girl – Geri Halliwell – has left. The remaining four come together from time to time to record and perform but each Spice Girl now produces solo records. Despite almost total contempt from the critics for their 'bubblegum pop', the Spice Girls have achieved as much popular success as The Beatles. Their biggest fan group is young girls aged from 8 to 12 who love their lively stage show and their songs' simple lyrics and bouncy rhythm.

Music of the new millennium?

English popular music is likely to continue to show a wide range of styles and influences. More 'boy bands' and 'girl groups' will come and go, big musicals will carry on being popular in the West End, and ethnic music – either from within or outside England – will exert a growing influence on those who write, and buy, the records we listen to. New technology will certainly continue to have a big effect on how music is produced and sold.

GLOSSARY

acoustic natural sound, not using electrification

album longer (1 hour or more) record or CD

amplification electronically increasing volume

anthem song, sometimes of a religious type, used on special occasions

avant garde new ideas, ahead of their time

ballads slow, romantic popular songs

baroque rich, complex type of seventeenth and eighteenth century music

beat time conduct, to show how fast the piece of music should be sung

cantata short piece of music for singers, sometimes accompanied by instruments

charts the 'top 20' or 'hit parade' of successful records

choral sung by a choir or group of singers

contralto woman singer who has a lower voice than a soprano

crooner male singer of romantic songs

digital electronic system making the sound or picture easier to read or listen to

DJs disc jockeys (those who play discs on radio, in clubs or at raves)

drum and bass electronic pop music with fast drum beats and loud bass

early music music from early periods (the Middle Ages to the eighteenth century)

genre type of music, art or literature

gospel style of choral religious music from the southern USA

hardcore electronic pop music, with a very fast beat and very few words

harmonic using two or more notes which sound pleasing together

hippie someone who follows the kind of life-style common in the 1960s when peace and love was the philosophy

hit parade list of the most popular records of the week

innovative introducing changes, new ideas or methods

instrumental piece of music performed with instruments and no voices

knight title given to a man who has performed some great service for his country; it allows him to put 'Sir' in front of his name

lyrics / lyricist words of a popular song; the one who writes them

masque special entertainment for the court in the seventeenth century, with music and dance based on a certain theme

mass piece of music which uses Christian prayers as words for singing

megaphone special machine to make your voice sound louder

to mob to gather round someone in a large crowd in order to see, touch or talk to him/her

oratorio piece of music, with a religious subject, written for singers and an orchestra

patron someone who gives money and support to artists, musicians, etc

rave large party held at night in a field or an empty building, with dancing to loud music

reggae type of pop music, which originated in the West Indies, with a very strong beat

remixers people who use a machine to rearrange and make new versions of records

samples electronic copying of part of a record in order to use it in another piece of music

scholarship money given by an organization to help someone pay for his/her studies

score the written version of a piece of music showing the notes which have to be played or sung

singles records which consist of just one or two short songs

soul / soulful type of music performed mainly by black Americans, expressing strong emotions

synthesizer electronic machine which produces computer-stored musical sounds

unaccompanied playing alone, without other musicians or instruments

versatile having many different skills

Taking it further

Suggested reading

Books

British and International Music Yearbook (annual), Rhinegold
    Publications
Everett, W, *The Beatles as Musicians*, OUP, 1999
Friedlander, P, *Rock and Roll: A Social History*, Westview Press, 1996
Gammond, P, *The Oxford Companion to Popular Music*, OUP, 1991
Helander, B, *The Rock Who's Who*, Schirmer Books, 1996
Larkin, C, *Encyclopedia of Popular Music*, Macmillan,
    (in eight volumes), 1998
Macan, E, *Rocking the Classics*, OUP, 1997
MacDonald, I, *Revolution in the Head*, 1995
Sadie, S (ed), *Grove's Concise Dictionary of Music*, 1988
Scholes, P, *The Oxford Companion to Music*, OUP, 1970

Magazines/journals

Opera (**http://www.opera.co.uk**)
Wire: adventures in modern music (**http://www.thewire.co.uk**)
Downbeat (for jazz, blues, etc): **http://www.downbeat.com**
Music magazine – produced by the BBC, e-mail:
    music.magazine@bbc.co.uk
Classical Music: e-mail: classical.music@rhinegold.co.uk,
    http://www.rhinegold.co.uk
Gramophone (for classical music):
    e-mail: gramophone@galleon.co.uk

Websites

Note that all of the record companies have websites containing
information about performers and new recordings (eg
http://www.emiclassics.com/artists).

http://www.grovemusic.com
http://www.biography.com
http://www.musicweb.uk.net/british.htm
http://www.musicroom.com

Suggested listening

In addition to the suggestions in the chapter above, you may like to try the following recordings. The labels *Naxos* and *Music for Pleasure* are good sources of relatively cheap classical recordings. For pop music, look out for *Best of ...* or *Greatest Hits* albums.

English performers of classical music

Kathleen Ferrier, *Blow the Wind Southerly: British Songs* (Decca)
Dennis Brain, *Mozart: Horn Concertos numbers 1-4* (Naxos)
Janet Baker, *Lieder: Mendelssohn, Schumann and Liszt* (EMI)
John Ogdon in Recital (Altarus)
John Lill, *Beethoven: The Piano Sonatas* (Decca)
Jacqueline du Pré, *Haydn and Boccherini: Cello Concertos* (EMI)
Kennedy, *Elgar's Violin Concerto* (EMI)

Folk

The Best of Fairport Convention (Island, 1972)
Fairport Convention, *Jewel in the Crown* (Woodworm, 1995)
The Best of Steeleye Span (Chrysalis, 1984)
Steeleye Span, *Original Masters* (BG, 1996)
Martin Carthy, *This is Martin Carthy* (Philips, 1972)
        Waterson Carthy (Topic, 1995)

Jazz

Johnny Dankworth, *What the Dickens!*
        Shakespeare and all that jazz
Courtney Pine, *In the Eyes of Creation* (Island, 1992)
        Back in the Day (Blue Thumb, 2000)

6 | TRADITIONS, FESTIVALS AND CUSTOMS

Despite its rich history, England does not formally celebrate any of its significant heroes or dates. There is no public holiday on St George's Day; the battles of Trafalgar and Waterloo are not officially marked, nor is the end of the Second World War; the birthdays of Shakespeare, Nelson and Wellington are not nationally commemorated. In fact, in a world league table of public holidays England is (jointly) last, a long way behind countries with stronger religious ties or a greater love of anniversaries. It is perhaps a reflection of our north European work ethic that we have just eight public holidays in the year: two at Christmas, one for New Year (and this was introduced only in the late 1970s), two at Easter and three Bank Holidays (so called, because these are days on which banks are legally closed).

National holidays		
Rank	**Country**	**Days per year**
1	Egypt	22
2	Hong Kong	17
3	Finland	15
4	Austria	14
5	Australia	13
	Japan	13
6	Canada	12
7	France	11
	The USA	11
8	Spain	10
	Northern Ireland	10
9	Germany	9
10	England/Scotland/Wales	8

[Reprinted by permission of *The Guardian* © The Guardian]

Christmas

The religious element of the Christmas holiday (and that of Easter as well) has weakened considerably since 1945. Church attendance – though still high compared with normal Sundays in the year – is steadily decreasing. Most English families see Christmas (or 'Xmas', as it is commonly abbreviated in writing) as a well-deserved, end-of-year break, a time to relax, have a good time – and spend money. The commercialism of Christmas grows stronger each year, with earlier and more advertising on TV, longer shop opening hours and higher spending by the public. Many factories and offices are shut between 24 December and 2 January, and many people take this opportunity to visit relations in other parts of the country.

Christmas traditions are changing too. Until the 1980s it was common to have carol singers going from street to street collecting for charities. Now this custom appears to be dying out, particularly in the cities; carols are more likely to be sung in formal settings such as church, school or town hall. Christmas decorations used to be limited to the inside of the home and the Christmas tree itself, but a more public show can be seen in some suburban streets where a house may be elaborately decorated with fairy lights and other seasonal displays. Decorated trees and hanging lights are also familiar sights now in most town centres.

The giving of presents (usually on Christmas morning) remains a custom, as does the big family lunch, which usually consists of a turkey and 'all the trimmings' (roast potatoes, a range of vegetables, cranberry sauce), followed by a Christmas pudding. The meal will often be accompanied by the pulling of crackers and the wearing of silly paper hats. After the meal, some families may settle down to play Christmas games (increasingly these are computer-based, but older board-games such as *Cluedo*, *Scrabble*, *Trivial Pursuit* and *Pictionary* remain popular). Other families may make a point of watching the Queen's traditional Christmas broadcast at 3.00 p.m. In fact, television is often the focal point of a family Christmas; consequently the TV channels compete with each other to show the films, soaps or sitcoms which can capture the biggest audience.

New Year's Eve

New Year's Eve is traditionally celebrated far less seriously in England that it is in Scotland. In the former it is not a special family occasion, and people may go to pubs, restaurants or friends for a party and to 'see in' the New Year. The most public manifestation of the event is the crowds which traditionally gather in London's Piccadilly Circus or Trafalgar Square in order to sing, dance and jump in the fountains (if allowed to) once midnight strikes. Although Christmas decorations remain in place until 6 January, the English return to work on 2 January, and there is no celebration of 'twelfth night', as there is in Southern Europe.

Other traditional festivals

St Valentine's Day (14 February)

On this day in England, as in many parts of the world, lovers of all ages send their sweethearts a card (sometimes anonymously) in order to express their love. The Personal Columns of the daily newspapers are full of such sentiments, with the writers often using funny, private nicknames for themselves and their loved ones.

Shrove Tuesday

Shrove Tuesday is the day before the beginning of Lent when it is traditional to eat pancakes. In some villages 'pancake races' (run by participants tossing pancakes in frying-pans) are held. There is no 'carnival' on this day, as there is in Catholic countries in Southern Europe and South America.

Pancake race

Mother's Day (or Mothering Sunday)

On the fourth Sunday in Lent, children traditionally give a card and a present to their mother. (This festival is more fully honoured than the less traditional Father's Day in the middle of June.)

Easter

The Christian religion marks this festival with church services. Many concerts featuring traditional sacred music, such as Handel's *Messiah*, are held at this time. English families also celebrate the idea of new birth by giving their children chocolate Easter eggs on Easter Sunday. During the weeks before Easter and on the preceding Friday (Good Friday), some bakers (and supermarkets) sell 'hot cross buns'; these are small sweet bread rolls containing currants, with a cross on top to represent the wooden cross on which Jesus died.

May Day

In England May Day was traditionally celebrated as the coming of spring, with dancing and ceremonies in many, mainly rural, communities. This has largely died out, though in Oxford, for example, the occasion is marked with hundreds of people (mostly young) gathering in the streets at dawn to listen to a choir greeting the spring from the top of Magdalen College Tower. The pubs in the city are traditionally open from 6.00 a.m. on that day. In some towns and villages too there may be dancing round the decorated 'maypole' and a display of morris-men (see **English folklore**, page 124). The May Day holiday (introduced by the Labour government in the 1970s as a way of marking Labour Day) is celebrated on the first Monday following 1 May.

Summer

There is a long gap in festive occasions between May Day and the next one, Hallowe'en, in October. How do communities in England fill the gap? Almost all villages and towns will organize during the summer a fête, flower-show or some other entertainment for local people. These occasions usually take place in the local church hall or on the village green or school grounds, and will feature games, competitions, music, a raffle, and sale of local produce (eg fruit, jams and vegetables provided by the people of the area).

Hallowe'en

In the past it was believed that on this night, 31 October, the dead would rise up from their graves. This idea is often celebrated now with parties at which guests dress up as ghosts or witches. More recently, the American custom of 'trick or treat' has become common. For this, children put on appropriate fancy dress and masks, and knock on doors saying 'Trick or Treat?' (but usually expecting the latter). A 'trick', if requested by the residents, would produce some kind of mild punishment such as being squirted with water or foam, while a 'treat' means sweets or money for the callers. The name Hallowe'en derives from All Hallows (Saints) Evening. The following day, 1 November (All Saints' Day), which is celebrated in Catholic countries, is not marked in any way in England.

Guy Fawkes' Day (5 November)

This is generally known as Bonfire Night, and marks the failure of the Gunpowder Plot in which Guy Fawkes and his fellow conspirators planned in 1605 to blow up the Houses of Parliament in London. Once it was common for a family with children to have its own bonfire, but now – largely for safety reasons – the bonfires are usually organized by local councils or communities. Two essential ingredients for the occasion are a 'guy' (a figure made of sticks and old clothes) put on top of the bonfire, and plenty of fireworks of all types for the crowds to enjoy.

Remembrance Day

Each year on the Sunday nearest to the 11 November, those killed in the First and Second World Wars are remembered in ceremonies and church services throughout Britain. In London there is an annual (televised) service at the Cenotaph in Whitehall which is attended by the Queen, the prime minister and other members of the government, parliamentary opposition and Royal Family. During this week many people choose to wear red paper poppies to remember those who died fighting for their country. (The area of Flanders, on the borders of Belgium and France, where many soldiers died in the First World War, is known for its poppy-fields). Traditionally a two-minute silence used to be held at 11.00 a.m. on Remembrance Day (the eleventh day of the eleventh month) in schools, shops, offices and factories across the country. Interestingly, this practice has been successfully reintroduced in recent years, perhaps because coverage in the media has made modern Britons more sharply aware of the sacrifices previous generations made for the country.

Unusual festivals and traditions

Gurning

The World Gurning Championships are held each September in Egremont in the Lake District, in north-west England. The tradition dates back to 1266. Gurning requires competitors to put their heads through a horse's collar and make the most horrible faces they can! The winner is the face which receives the most applause.

Cheese-rolling

This takes place on Cooper's Hill in Gloucestershire each May. The tradition is over two hundred years old, and involves competitors chasing a large round local cheese (Double Gloucester) down a steep hill and trying to catch it. In 1997, there were serious injuries to thirty-three people so the race was banned for the following year!

Minehead May Day

On this day a hobby-horse (a toy made from a long stick, with a horse's head at one end) dances round the town of Minehead in Somerset, in the west of England. It is followed by musicians, singing 'The Hobbyhorse Song', and asking local people to contribute money to charity. If they do not give generously, they are attacked by the horse's head and tail!

Bognor Regis Birdman

This annual competition, which is held on the coast of Sussex, southern England, is relatively new (from 1974). It offers a cash prize of £25,000 to anyone who can fly over 46 m out to sea from a platform. About twenty thousand people come each September to watch the competitors in their crazy flying machines – most of which soon crash into the water.

The World Lying Championships

These were originated by a nineteenth-century pub-owner and take place each November in Wasdale, Cumbria, in north-west England. Each competitor is allowed between two and five minutes to persuade the judges of their ability to tell a convincing 'tall story'. One interesting rule of the game is that no politicians or lawyers are allowed to take part, as it was felt they would have an unfair advantage!

Ethnic festivals

As an increasingly multi-cultural country, England now sees other ethnic communities marking their own festivals, notably Diwali (for Hindus) in the autumn, and Chinese New Year (in early February), with parades in certain areas of the big cities (eg Chinatown in London's Soho area), street decorations, fireworks and religious services.

Sporting events

These have their own special place in the English calendar and in the hearts of a large section of the population. The year is punctuated by annual sporting occasions such as the Six-Nations rugby tournament beginning in January (involving England, Scotland, Wales, a (joint) Irish team, France and Italy). For horse-racing fans there is the Cheltenham Gold Cup in March, the Grand National at Aintree near Liverpool, and the Derby at Epsom in June. The Oxford–Cambridge University Boat Race takes place on the Thames in the spring. This is followed by the FA (Football Association) Cup Final in May, the Wimbledon tennis championships at the end of the June, and the five-day-long cricket Test matches throughout the summer (weather permitting!). In July there is the British motor-racing Grand Prix at the Silverstone circuit in Northamptonshire and the British Open golf championship (which can take place in England or Scotland). Sport has a powerful hold on the English mind, and consequently, millions of people each year attend these events or follow them in the press and on TV.

Fund-raising events

Rapidly becoming a tradition in the yearly round is the fund-raising appeal for donations to charities. Some of these have now become huge televised events which raise millions of pounds, for example the Children in Need appeal in the autumn, when the public both participate in events and phone in to pledge money for the chosen charity. One biennial appeal which has really caught the public's imagination and has also raised a huge amount of money for good causes, is Red Nose day (or Comic Relief), so-called because of the clown's traditionally red nose. This TV event is presented by comedians and consists of comedy routines and sketches, together with items about the work the charities are doing, mainly in Africa and other less-developed countries.

Artistic festivals

Almost every town or city in England now seems to have its own festival. Such events usually take place in the summer and feature one or more of the arts, with exhibitions, shows and performances taking place in local halls, churches or arts centres. Some of these festivals started big, while over the years others have grown to achieve widespread fame and popularity. Some of the better-known are mentioned below.

The 'Proms'

The word comes from the French 'promenade' meaning a walk, and is used because a section of the audience at the concerts may stand or (if there is room!) walk up and down. The Promenade Concerts first started in 1895 and moved to their current venue, the Royal Albert Hall (London) in 1942. They are now more popular than ever, with a huge worldwide TV audience for the famous 'Last Night' in September on which traditional English music is played (see page 89), and there is much audience participation and good humour. The concerts (over seventy in all) always feature classical music, though part of the philosophy of the Proms is to introduce contemporary music, and indeed to commission new works. Other types of music (opera, jazz, film scores, gospel, electro-acoustic) have also been introduced. Many of the concerts are given by the BBC Symphony Orchestra; the BBC sponsors the Proms and broadcasts all of the concerts 'live' on radio, and some on TV.

Stratford-upon-Avon

It would be surprising if the birthplace of William Shakespeare did not have an annual theatre festival. The Royal Shakespeare Company (or RSC, as the company is commonly known) performs a selection of Shakespeare's plays there each year (from March to October). The RSC has three theatres in Stratford beside the River Avon. The newest and smallest one, called the Other Place, is where new works or new versions of classic plays (not only by Shakespeare) are performed.

The theatre world and the Stratford City Council had a shock in 2001 when the RSC announced that it wished to knock down the oldest of the three theatres, the Royal Shakespeare Theatre – built in 1932 – in order to build a new one, together with training, rehearsal and education centres. The plans have yet to be approved.

The RSC also has a base in London, at the Barbican Centre, where its season runs from October to May.

It also takes its plays on extensive tours of Britain and the rest of the world. Many of England's greatest modern actors and directors first came to the public's notice while working at Stratford: Peter Brook, Peter Hall and Adrian Noble among the directors, while the list of great actors includes Glenda Jackson, Jeremy Irons, Ian Holm, Alan Rickman and Juliet Stevenson.

Cheltenham

This handsome Regency city in the Cotswolds is the setting for not one, but two annual artistic festivals (or three, if we include the horse-racing festival in March!): these are the two-week music festival in July and the ten-day literary festival in October. Each attracts well-known international artists as well as a lot of music or literature enthusiasts.

Glyndebourne

This is another music festival which takes place in a delightful setting, in this case the Sussex Downs, near the quiet village of Glynde (near the county town of Lewes). An attractive modern auditorium has recently been built to replace the older one which was first used for this opera festival in 1934. Glyndebourne has a reputation as a festival where new works as well as traditional operas are performed. It is almost equally famous for another performance which takes place during the especially long interval. Members of the audience, elegantly dressed in dinner jackets and evening dresses, move swiftly to reserve their places in the beautiful gardens surrounding the auditorium. Here they will sit on rugs, sip champagne or wine and have a delicious meal, which they have usually brought themselves in hampers.

Glyndebourne

The Three Choirs festival

As its name suggests, this festival mainly features choral work, but new and traditional orchestral music is also a regular part of the programme. In August each year, the festival is held in the home city of one of the three choirs, that is Gloucester, Hereford or Worcester. The composer, Edward Elgar (see Chapter Five), did a lot to establish the reputation of the festival in its early years.

Aldeburgh

Less well-known than Glyndebourne, Aldeburgh, a small east coast fishing town, is the site of England's other great classical music and opera festival. It has achieved this fame largely for two reasons: its founders and its setting. Benjamin Britten, probably England's finest composer of the twentieth century, and his close friend Peter Pears, a leading opera singer, established the festival in 1948. Later, an old maltings (a building where malt is prepared for making beer) near the remote and beautiful coastline of Suffolk was converted into an elegant concert hall. This building and its setting is the second reason for Aldeburgh's success. In addition to the festival, the Britten-Pears School of Advanced Musical Studies has also been established in Aldeburgh.

Glastonbury

What greater contrast could there be with Glyndebourne and Aldeburgh than this massive, loud and muddy tribute to the joys of a different kind of music! The four-day Glastonbury Festival takes place in June on a large area of land owned by a Somerset farmer, Michael Eavis. The festival began on a relatively small scale in 1970, but has grown each year to become a huge event, attended in the year 2000 by over 100,000 music fans. However, this growth in numbers led the organizers to cancel the 2001 festival since they were worried about the dangers of overcrowding. In 2000 thousands of fans got into the festival site illegally by climbing over, or tunnelling under, the fences. Over the years, the festival has expanded its range. Now there is not only rock music, but a wide range of folk, ethnic, jazz and dance music, as well as circus and theatre events. The audience too has changed to include music fans of all ages, nationalities and backgrounds. Of course, outdoor festivals are at the mercy of the weather. In one very wet June, the festival site became a sea of mud, but the bands played on!

Cambridge

This famous university town is very busy in July since it hosts two festivals then. One is the Folk Festival which has been running since 1964 and continues to attract a wide range of international performers. The other is the international Film Festival which has been going since 1980. It not only shows new films, but also has talks by leading actors and directors, and retrospectives of the work of some of the great names of film.

Reading

The city of Reading has an important place in the English music world, since it hosts two important festivals: the rock music festival in August, and WOMAD (World of Music, Arts and Dance) in July. Though less famous than Glastonbury, each festival attracts big – but very different – audiences, with the rock festival also having a reputation for indie and alternative music. WOMAD was established by the rock singer, Peter Gabriel, in 1982, and moved to the banks of the River Thames in Reading in 1990. About twenty thousand visitors come and listen to the sixty or so groups each year; WOMAD provides an opportunity for international musicians (playing a very wide variety of music) to find new audiences in this country.

Notting Hill

This is known as a carnival, rather than a festival, because its style and content are more exotic than typically English. It is organized by London's Caribbean community and can be compared to a big street party, with entertainment, food, drink, music, dancing, a big parade and competitions for calypsos, costumes and steel bands. The carnival takes place in the central part of London every August, and, like all festivals, is the result of long and careful planning. The police are involved in this too, both to organise the traffic (several streets are closed to traffic during the carnival), and to help avoid trouble (there are inevitably cases of pickpocketing and fighting). It has been estimated that the carnival attracts over 2 million visitors and sightseers over the weekend – that's some party!

English folklore

Like most countries England has a rich folklore, though the traditions which live on today tend to seem quaint rather than an integral part of the everyday lives of English people. Tourists, of course, are always attracted by the traditional images of England, such as Beefeaters, the Tower of London, the Changing of the Guard or the Queen's Opening of Parliament. The English are well-known for their great ability to present the pageantry of history and to stage big ceremonial events.

A good example of a more ordinary popular tradition is morris-dancing. This developed from ancient pagan practices and its original intention was to frighten away evil spirits. The dance is performed in groups of six (usually men), and the dancers, who wear white, have bells on their legs, and carry handkerchiefs and sticks, can be seen on many a village green, in town centres, or outside pubs in the summer, usually as the entertainment to accompany a fête, festival or official celebration.

Morris dancers

Superstitions too appear to have less force now than they once did, probably as a result of mass media and the spread of education. It is rare nowadays to meet someone who truly believes that, for example, Friday the 13th, walking under a ladder, breaking a mirror or seeing a black cat will really bring bad luck. Yet there is a flourishing network of believers in ghosts and UFOs, so perhaps the English people's traditional interest in the supernatural is not quite lost.

Crop circles

Crop circles are becoming established as a new item of English folklore. These are circular areas in fields of crops which overnight (by magic?) become flat. Many photos have been taken of them (from the air), and the circles – often in complex patterns – can certainly look beautiful. Some people believe they are made by creatures from outer space, some that winds are the cause, while others think that clever people create them by using ordinary equipment such as string and a long piece of wood!

As old English traditions and folk rituals fade, some new, commercially-based customs seem to have replaced them. This trend has certainly affected the traditional English Sunday. It is far more common now to go to a supermarket, a car boot sale or a sporting event on a Sunday than it is to go to church or to spend a quiet day at home with the family. These changes have meant, of course, that many people (who used to enjoy a free Sunday) now have to work on that day, but on the whole the English welcome this change, remembering how dull an English Sunday could be! As we have seen, the general pattern of work and leisure in England has changed over the last thirty years. Although there is a greater variety of 'things to do' in or out of home, many older people regret the loss of closeness and greater sense of community that were once found in villages, towns and city districts, when they used to come together on traditional occasions each year, whether for purposes of religion or entertainment. England has to a large extent lost that feeling (except perhaps in the fields of sport or 'live' performance) and can only recapture it now artificially when national events are broadcast on television.

GLOSSARY

all the trimmings the extra things that it is traditional to have for a special meal or occasion

audience participation parts of a show or concert where the spectators are asked to sing, wave, clap their hands, etc

auditorium part of a public hall or building where the audience sits

bonfire planned large outdoor fire

calypso song from the Caribbean which deals with a current topic

car boot sale outdoor sale where people sell things that they no longer want (from the backs of their cars)

carol Christian religious song sung at Christmas

Cenotaph monument built in honour of soldiers killed in a war who are buried elsewhere

Christmas pudding hot, sweet dish like a dark fruit cake

conspirators people involved in a secret plan to do something illegal

Cotswolds pretty range of hills in Gloucestershire

crackers tubes of coloured paper that make a bang when pulled open by two people; they usually contain a paper hat, a joke and a small present

dinner jacket black jacket worn by men with a bow-tie at formal occasions

fairy lights small coloured electric lights used for decoration

fancy dress clothes worn at parties to make you look like a different character

fête outdoor entertainment, usually arranged to make money for a special purpose

fund-raising appeal request to the public to give money to a charity

gospel style of religious singing, popular among African Americans

hamper large basket with a cover, to carry food in

indie (music) music played by bands that are new, or produced by small independent companies

Lent in the Christian church, the period (of forty days) leading up to Easter

pagan holding religious beliefs that are not part of any of the world's main religions

pageants big, colourful events or traditional ceremonies involving people wearing special costumes

pancake thin, flat round cake, made in a pan from flour, eggs, and milk

Personal Column section of a newspaper containing private messages

pickpocketing stealing money from people's pockets, especially in crowded places

poppy red flower, with black seeds

quaint interesting or attractive in an unusual or old-fashioned way

raffle kind of lottery in which numbered tickets are sold, and those with the chosen numbers win prizes

Regency style of the period 1811–1820, when George, Prince of Wales, was regent (ie ruled the country in place of the king, his father)

retrospective public showing of the work an artist or film-maker has done in the past

rug large, square piece of material, made of wool, used as a covering

sacred holy, religious

sitcom TV situation comedy programme

steel bands groups (originally from the West Indies) who play music on drums made from empty metal containers

Test Match international cricket match between two teams, played over five days

UFOs Unidentified Flying Objects seen in the sky

Taking it further

The best thing you can do is to come over to England and visit some of the places or attend some of the events mentioned above. If you cannot do that, then here are some other ways to find out more ...

Suggested reading

Simpson, Jacqueline and Roud, Steve, *A Dictionary of English Folklore*, OUP, 2001

Websites

http://www.visitbritain.com   The official website of the British Tourist Authority

http://www.atuk.co.uk   For a guide to travel and tourism around Britain

http://www.chillisauce.co.uk/bizarre_festivals   For further details of those unusual traditions

http://www.bbc.co.uk/proms   Gives details of the Promenade concerts

http://www.efestivals.co.uk   All you need to know about summer pop festivals

http://www.nottinghillcarnival.net.uk/infohome

http://www.glastonburyfestivals.co.uk

http://www.womad.org

http://www.cadenza.org/links   For information about classical music

http://www.shef/ac.uk/english/natcect   For details of the National Centre for English Cultural Tradition

7 | CREATIVITY IN CONTEMPORARY ENGLAND

Two major areas of English creativity – music and literature – have already been discussed, but there are several other fields in which the English have left their mark on the world and for which they continue to be famous. It is true that other nations have overtaken the English in areas where they used to be strong, for example, in the manufacturing of ships, cars, motorbikes, and even in most sports. However, the English have always shown the ability to 'reinvent' themselves, and to use their creative ability in new aspects of life. This chapter will look at some of these areas, and will include design, broadcasting, cinema and cookery. But first, a look back …

Some historical background

During the period of its great industrial expansion in the eighteenth and nineteenth centuries, England produced many inventors whose names are still familiar. Thanks to many of their inventions, England became the first country to experience an Industrial Revolution. This helped it to develop its economy and its military power, thus making it the most influential country in the world during the reign of Queen Victoria (1837–1901) and up until the First World War. Here are the names of some great inventors: do you recognize any of them?

- **John Harrison** (1693–1776) invented 'time-keepers' which could be used by sailors to keep both 'local' time at sea and the time at another fixed point, such as their home port. The story of how Harrison finally managed to win the prize announced in 1714 for the first person to 'find longitude' is one of the great stories of human invention – and was well described in the popular book, *Longitude,* by Dava Sobel in 1999.

Stephenson's locomotive

- **Richard Arkwright** (1732–1792) invented a machine which used water power (a water-wheel) to spin cotton. This development in the eighteenth century was at the heart of the Industrial Revolution in the eighteenth century and helped to make the English textile industry the most important in the world for many years to come.

- **Edward Jenner** (1749–1823) discovered vaccination (injection to prevent disease).

- **George Stephenson** (1781–1848) designed some of the first steam trains and in 1825 was also the first to construct a public railway (between Stockton and Darlington in the north-east of England). The locomotive (called *The Rocket*) was the first to run at a speed (30 miles per hour/48 km/h) greater than walking pace. These inventions started the huge and rapid development of railways in England in the nineteenth century.

- **Michael Faraday** (1791–1867) discovered electro-magnetic induction, which led to the development of the electric dynamo.

- **Charles Babbage** (1792–1871) was the 'grandfather' of the modern calculator and computer, in that he was the first to invent a machine to do complex mathematical calculations.

- **Isambard Kingdom Brunel** (1806–1869), who was England's greatest ever engineer, designed the first steamship to cross the Atlantic and was also the first to use propellers on a ship making that journey. He also designed the famous Clifton Suspension

Bridge in Bristol and much of the Great Western Railway.

- **Rowland Hill** (1795–1879) invented the postage stamp in 1840.
- **Joseph Swan** (1828–1914) was, according to the English, the first to invent the electric light bulb. He did this in 1848, and finally managed to show its use to the public in Newcastle in 1879. However, Americans claim that Thomas Edison beat Swan to it.
- **William Fox Talbot** (1800–1877) led the development of photography in the 1830s.
- **Robert Whitehead** (1828–1905) invented the torpedo in 1866.
- **J P Knight** invented traffic lights in 1868.
- **Sir Francis Galton** (1822–1911) in 1884 developed the process of fingerprints to help police or lawyers to identify people (dead or alive).

Technology of the twentieth and twenty-first centuries

It is true to say that many inventions in the modern world come from the desire or need to give one's country an advantage in espionage or war. In the last century England certainly had a few inventions of this type, but also others where the inspiration was purely to make life easier or better in some way. So far, over 70 Britons have won Nobel Prizes for their work, a number second only to the United States.

Famous inventions		
Inventor	**Date**	**Invention**
Frank Whittle	1930	The jet engine
Percy Shaw	1934	Cats' eyes (reflectors on roads)
Barnes Wallis	1943	The bouncing bomb (used in the Second World War)
Alan Turing	1947	Artificial intelligence (via computers)
Geoffrey De Havilland	1949	The Comet (the first jet airliner)

Christopher Cockerell	1955	The hovercraft
Clive Sinclair	1966	Pocket calculator, pocket TV, the 'C5' electric car
Francis Crick (and James Watson, an American)	1973	The structure of DNA, the chemical in plant and animal cells that carries genetic information
Patrick Steptoe	1977	In-vitro fertilization (creating life outside the body)
James Dyson	1978	The 'bag-less' vacuum cleaner
Tim Berners-Lee	1989	The World Wide Web (and then in 1990 the first browser to help you read Web documents)
Trevor Baylis	1991	The clockwork radio

Although England has been first with many new industries and engineering achievements, it has also been the first to experience problems when these things become old or out of date, as exemplified by our railways and underground (or 'tube') system, which now require great investment and modernization. Several industries for which England was once famous throughout the world – coal, steel, shipbuilding and textiles – have declined rapidly since the Second World War, as other countries were able to produce the same things more cheaply and quickly.

Nevertheless, England still has many areas of technology where its expertise is highly valued.

Motor racing

Many of the Formula 1 teams, although some are sponsored by foreign manufacturers, are based in central England. Williams, Arrow, Jordan, and McLaren all have their workshops and test centres here. Why? Because they value the high standard of work done by the experienced English designers and mechanics.

Car manufacture

This is in a similar position to motor racing. It continues successfully, even though the factories are owned by foreign companies – Ford, Toyota, Nissan, Honda and BMW all have big factories in Britain. The well-known English car names such as Jaguar, Rover, Aston-Martin, Rolls-Royce, Landrover and the new Mini are produced in the same factories as in previous years, but now the owners are American or German. England still has a few small companies producing truly English cars, for example, the Morgan, the TVR sports car, and the Reliant Robin three-wheeler.

Engineering

At the top of England's exports list come engineering and transport machinery and electronic equipment. These manufactured products need engineers and designers, most of whom come from British universities. England maintains a strong reputation throughout the world for the quality of its higher education, including the engineering departments of universities like Lancaster, Cambridge, East Anglia, Oxford and Liverpool.

Key research is also being carried out in other fields: biological sciences, business and economics, and social sciences. University College, the London School of Economics, Sussex, Newcastle and Bristol Universities all have a very high standing in these areas. But universities suffer from the same problem mentioned later in this chapter, which is that some of the best people are regularly lost to the higher salaries and the warmer climates of the USA.

Looking back across the twentieth century, there have been some heroic achievements in the use or design of engineering on land or sea, and in the air:

- **Alcock and Brown**: on 14 June 1919, John Alcock (pilot) and Arthur Brown (navigator) made the first non-stop crossing of the Atlantic, from Newfoundland in Canada to Clifden in Ireland; it took 16 hours, 28 minutes.
- **Amy Johnson** (1903–1941): Johnson was England's best-known woman pilot: she flew alone from London to Australia in 1930.

- **The Everest Expedition**: on the day of Queen Elizabeth's coronation in 1953, news came that a British group led by an ex-army officer, John Hunt, had been the first to climb Mount Everest, the world's highest mountain.

- **Donald Campbell** (1921–1967): he was, like his father, a racing driver who wanted to go faster on land and water than anyone had ever gone before. He achieved both records in the 1950s and 1960s. He died when his specially designed speed-boat, *Bluebird*, crashed on Coniston Water (a lake in north-west England) where he was trying to break another record.

- **Concorde**: this plane was designed and built by the British and French together. It was the first passenger jet to fly faster than the speed of sound, and has been in service since 1976.

- **The Mini**: this has probably become the most successful British car of all time. Small, cheap and fun to drive, the Mini was designed by Sir Alec Issigonis (who was born in Turkey) and was first on sale to the public in 1959.

- **The Channel Tunnel**: another joint Franco-British project. The idea of a road or rail link, which had first been suggested early in the nineteenth century, was finally achieved in 1994, at a cost of over £8 billion.

- **Thrust SSC**: this was the British-designed Supersonic Car which in 1997 Andy Green drove to a new land-speed record of 763 miles per hour (1228 km/h).

Entrepreneurs and Dot Com

The two best-known entrepreneurs in England today are probably **Richard Branson** and **Anita Roddick**. Branson (b. 1950) set up the Virgin record company in 1970, selling it in 1992; he started the Virgin Atlantic Airline in 1984, and Virgin Rail in 1996. He is also famous for having crossed the Atlantic (1987) and the Pacific (1991) by balloon. Roddick (b. 1942) is best-known for the popular and successful Body Shop company which she set up in 1976. She had noticed a public interest in alternative medicine, the environment, and animal rights, and put these ideas together in the sale of beauty products made from natural materials, many of them from less-developed countries.

In the late 1990s there was a sudden rush of interest in the new 'dot com' companies (Internet service sites) set up by young English entrepreneurs. For some, the bubble soon burst, and the companies did not survive. One company which has survived and is still doing well is lastminute.com. Its idea was to buy unsold aeroplane seats, theatre tickets, gifts and hotel bookings and sell them on the internet at a reduced price to people who always left such things to the 'last minute'. The company's two owners, Brent Hoberman and Martha Lane Fox, have become millionaires. The fact that they were young, clever and attractive helped to bring their company both the financial backing and the publicity it needed to get started. Now lastminute.com is well-established throughout Europe.

Fashion

What do you associate with these names: Moss Bros? Burberry? Barbour? Clarks? Aquascutum? Jaeger? Liberty? Gieves and Hawkes? You are right if you know that all of these names stand for high-quality, and highly-priced, clothes (except Clarks which sell middle-priced shoes). It is perhaps no surprise that in a climate where it rains a lot, the English have always been good at producing rain-wear as well as warm woollen clothes, using the wool from sheep raised on those damp English hill-sides! Though the English still have a certain reputation for traditional clothes or 'classic tailoring', they are now challenging the French and the Italians with bright young designers and attractive new styles.

Hardy Amies and Norman Hartnell

The two best-known British designers of an earlier period were **Hardy Amies** (b. 1909) and **Norman Hartnell** (1901–1979). Both worked in Paris before setting up their own businesses, and each was later appointed dressmaker to the British Royal Family who were known for their conservative style. This image began to change in the 1980s when Princess Diana wore glamorous new styles created by younger English designers such as Jasper Conran, Bruce Oldfield and Catherine Walker.

Mary Quant and Zandra Rhodes

In the 1960s, something happened to British fashion to make it more daring and truly popular. The top designers of the time were **Mary Quant** (b. 1934) and **Zandra Rhodes** (b. 1940). It was Quant who – along with the 'supermodels' of the time, Twiggy and Jean Shrimpton – helped to make the mini-skirt so popular. Mary Quant has now developed an international company, selling clothes, textiles and cosmetics. In the 1960s both of these designers had shops on or near the King's Road in Chelsea, and this helped to make the area a target for all those who wished to buy the latest fashions. As lively and stylish clothes became affordable for all young people, so new shops and designers emerged.

Vivienne Westwood and Katherine Hamnett

Two designers who began to achieve success in the 1970s and are now big names in British fashion are **Vivienne Westwood** (b. 1941) and **Katharine Hamnett** (b. 1947). Westwood set up a boutique (clothes shop) called Let it Rock in the King's Road in 1971 with her then partner, **Malcolm McLaren**. At first they sold 'retro' 1950s-style clothes to a new generation, but in 1976 turned to selling punk gear such as ripped T-shirts, big boots, and trousers decorated with pins and chains. Since 1983 Westwood has worked under her own name and has become a very influential designer. She is known for her witty, eccentric style and her use of historical and artistic sources for her inspiration, for example in her ranges of clothes based on the Italian rococo style of art or on the French revolution.

Like many others who have become successful designers, Katharine Hamnett studied at St Martin's School of Art in London (now called Central St Martin's College of Art and Design). In 1979 she set up her own fashion house, and has become best-known for her ready-to-wear fashions which are often based on work-clothes, and for bringing environmental issues into fashion, for example, with T-shirts printed with slogans such as 'Choose Life'.

The British Fashion Council

In 1983, the British Fashion Council (BFC) was formed, partly to organize British Fashion Week which usually takes place in February. This is a great opportunity for both new and established designers to show their latest styles, win orders and catch the attention of the big clothes shops and fashion houses. In 2001, there were fifty-two separate collections being shown during the week, compared with only fifteen in 1994. Interestingly, twenty-six of the designers presenting their collections were graduates of the same college – St Martin's.

Designer of the Year

The British Fashion Council introduced this award in 1984. Previous English winners include:

1984: Katharine Hamnett

1985: Betty Jackson

1986: Jasper Conran

1987, 1994 and 1995: John Galliano

1990 and 1991: Vivienne Westwood

1996 and 2001: Alexander McQueen

1999 and 2000: Hussein Chalayan

Some of the newer names above have already made their mark beyond England: **John Galliano** (b. 1960) has worked for the famous French fashion houses, Givenchy and Christian Dior. **Alexander McQueen** (b. 1969) followed Galliano to Paris, and took over from him as chief designer at Givenchy in 1996. He now has his own label. **Stella McCartney** (b. 1971), daughter of ex-Beatle Paul, was for a time a designer for the French fashion house, Chloé, but is now working for Gucci. Add to these three names those of other well-known designers such as **George Davies** (who set up the Next chain of shops), **Paul Smith**, **Georgina Godley** and **Ozwald Boateng**, and it is clear that England has an increasing worldwide reputation in popular fashion. Madonna, Kate Winslet and Gwynneth Paltrow, have all appeared at glamorous events in English-made designs.

Design

It is not only in fashion that England has brilliant designers. However, many designers in other fields have found that there is no longer a big enough manufacturing base in Britain to need or pay for their designs. For example, **Jonathan Ive**, one of England's top designers, went to California a few years ago and found greater fame there as Head of Design for Apple Computers, for whom he designed the new iMac computers. **Tom Dixon**, who designed the popular 'S-chair', designs stylish furniture which is often produced in Italy. His company, Eurolounge, also makes the plastic 'Jack lamp' which can be bent into different shapes. Another English designer, **Jasper Morrison**, has worked designing trams in Germany, and kitchen products for the Italian company Alessi.

Yet there is still much that is happening in England; for example, the **Design Museum**, which opened in 1989 on the south bank of the Thames in London. This runs exhibitions of twentieth and twenty-first century design items and also has a Study Centre where school and university students can learn about the process from design to manufacture. The **Millennium Dome**, which was situated further east along the Thames, closed in 2001, but one of its best aspects was the collection of one thousand innovative products nearly all of which were designed and made in England.

Each year the Arts Foundation awards a prize to the best British design in various fields: household products, publishing, theatre, landscape, jewellery, and so on. England is also very strong in graphic design, partly because it has large and successful publishing and broadcasting industries which constantly require art-work from graphic designers. An interesting example of a graphic designer who has gone on to work in a related field is **Nick Park** (b. 1959), the animator whose company, Aardman Animations, based in Bristol, has won three Oscars for its short comic films (for example, *The Wrong Trousers* and *A Close Shave*) about the inventor Wallace and his dog, Gromit.

Sir Terence Conran

Perhaps the guru of English design is **Sir Terence Conran** (b. 1931). In 1964 he opened his first shop on the Fulham Road in London; it was called Habitat, a name now familiar throughout Britain. It was soon a success, and was joined by other well-known clothing firms – Next, BHS and Mothercare – to form The Storehouse Group. The secret of Habitat's enduring success is to sell well-designed and affordable domestic products (furniture, lamps, carpets, kitchenware, etc) in plain styles and attractive colours. Conran's philosophy is this: 'Good design can make everyday objects both a pleasure to use and to behold'. In the last forty years he, more than anyone else, has changed the way English houses look inside. Sir Terence's group also put up the money for The Design Museum to be built – it does contain several of his own creations! Sir Terence's son, Jasper, is now a successful designer too, but mainly of clothes.

Visitor attractions

It is not surprising that the English, with their strong sense of tradition, history and attention to detail, are good at creating museums. London has seen some of the most exciting recent developments in design and innovation in museums and galleries, many of which have new 'hi-tech' rooms. In the 'Taking it further' section at the end of this chapter you will find a list of some of the best, but below are details of a couple of new attractions which you may not have heard of:

- London's newest attraction is the **Millennium Wheel**. It is owned and run by British Airways, and is commonly known as the 'London Eye'; this impressive 138-m high structure, situated on the Thames almost opposite the Houses of Parliament, gives visitors a half-hour ride and offers wonderful views over London and the surrounding area. It was designed by English architects Marks Barfield.

- **The Eden Project**, in Cornwall in south-west England, recreates below ground a sheltered micro-climate in which the natural worlds typical of South America, South Africa, the Mediterranean and California can grow and develop. The project was based on a huge quarry but now covers a much wider area where the 'biomes', or vast covered greenhouses, have been constructed. The largest is 100 m across and 45 m high. The project's architects were one of England's best-known firms, Nicholas Grimshaw and Partners. The Eden Project opened in 2000 and is already attracting a huge number of visitors.

Millennium Wheel

TV

The BBC (the British Broadcasting Corporation) is one of the most respected media organizations in the world. Its name still stands for truthful reporting, fairness and impartiality. It is often the case that where there is a revolution or a war, both sides of the conflict will listen to the BBC to get a true and balanced picture of what is happening in their country.

The ambition of a lot of clever, creative young people in Britain is to establish a career in the broadcasting media. Over many years this has resulted in a remarkably high number of memorable programmes and series produced by the BBC and its two terrestrial rivals, Independent Television (or ITV) and Channel Four (the satellite TV channels have still to produce anything as lasting). These programmes bring useful income since they are often sold to other TV stations and shown all over the world. They can perhaps be grouped into three main areas:

Comedy

English TV has had great international success with a number of comedy programmes. Many of these took their inspiration from some wonderful BBC radio comedy programmes of the 1950s, such as *Hancock's Half Hour, Round the Horne*, and *The Goons* (in which the future fim star Peter Sellers first made his name). Since then, most of the best comedy series have been on TV. Are any of these familiar to you: *Steptoe and Son, Dad's Army, Monty Python's Flying Circus, Till Death Us Do Part, Yes Minister, Fawlty Towers, Mr Bean, Only Fools and Horses, Blackadder, Men Behaving Badly, Absolutely Fabulous*?

There have been attempts to make 'big screen' films of many of these series, but only those made by the Monty Python team (*Monty Python and the Holy Grail, The Life of Brian, The Meaning of Life*), and *Bean* in 1997 have achieved any real success. However, **John Cleese** (from *Monty Python*) and **Rowan Atkinson** (Mr Bean) have become internationally known as stars of comedy. Richard Curtis, who started writing for TV's *Not the Nine O'Clock News* and *Blackadder*, has gone on to even greater fame (and wealth) as the writer of the successful English film comedies, *Four Weddings and a Funeral, Bean* and *Notting Hill*.

TV has also made stars of many comedians too: Benny Hill, Frankie Howerd, Tommy Cooper and, more recently, Harry Enfield and Paul Merton, have all owed their wider fame to this medium.

Documentaries

The most famous name in this area of British television is David Attenborough (b. 1926), the brother of the equally famous Richard (see later in this chapter). David is a presenter and maker of BBC programmes about nature in all forms and in all parts of the world – from plants and insects to fish, birds, and wild animals. His willingness to get as close as possible to the animals and his ability to communicate his enthusiasm have made his programmes hugely popular, and have helped him win many TV awards. His best-known series have been *Life on Earth, The Living Planet, The Private Life of Plants* and *The Life of Birds*.

English TV also has a reputation for powerfully realistic documentaries, and over the years many of these have caused controversy because they have revealed weaknesses or hidden facts about institutions in Britain. Examples have been programmes about the Royal Family, police, drug use, hospitals, schools and Britain's role in Northern Ireland.

Drama

BBC and the other independent terrestrial channels have produced many memorable drama series since the 1960s. One that many people still remember well is ITV's *The Avengers*, a stylish and cleverly written comedy-thriller which showed the adventures of an English gentleman, John Steed, and his beautiful female colleague, an expert in judo. Another was the BBC's *Dr Who*. This was a science fiction fantasy series (1963–1989) which was originally made for children, but which soon proved popular with the whole family. Dr Who travelled through time and space in a police call-box, 'The Tardis', doing battle with his enemies at each point. A third fantasy drama, *The Prisoner*, made by ITV in the late 1960s, still has a big fan-club which meets each year to discuss and re-enact scenes from the series. It was a very exciting, surreal series which was on one level about a secret agent kept prisoner in a village, but on another it raised questions about man's search for true freedom in a conformist society.

Costume drama

Over the years BBC and ITV have found markets abroad for their successful adaptations of classic novels. TV companies are skilful in making the adaptations look right, with great attention paid to costume and setting, using older English towns and country houses as the location for stories from the eighteenth or nineteenth centuries. One would expect the work of Shakespeare and Dickens to be regularly revisited, but other writers too have had their work successfully recreated on television:

Jane Austen: all her novels have now been adapted for TV, but the BBC's adaptation of *Pride and Prejudice* in 1995 was a particular success both at home and abroad.

John Galsworthy: he won the Nobel Prize for Literature in 1931. His best-known work, *The Forsyte Saga*, about the fortunes of an early-twentieth-century family, was adapted for TV by the BBC in 1969 and by ITV in 2002.

Anthony Trollope: two whole series of his novels (general titles *The Barchester Chronicles* and *The Pallisers*) about middle-class Victorian life were adapted by the BBC in the 1980s, and more recently his novel, *The Way We Live Now,* scored another success for the BBC.

Evelyn Waugh: his famous novel about an aristocratic family, *Brideshead Revisited*, was very popular when it was filmed in the 1980s, and confirmed the view that the public often liked to see stories about the lives of the rich and elegant!

Paul Scott: his quartet of books about the British in India, also made for TV in the 1980s as *The Jewel in the Crown*, found similar popularity and critical success, winning many TV awards.

Crime series

Detective and spy stories (see page 61) have been a rich source for TV companies looking for a trusted formula: in particular the detectives created by **Agatha Christie** (Miss Marple and Hercule Poirot), **Ruth Rendell** (Inspector Wexford), **John Le Carré** (George Smiley) and **Colin Dexter** (Inspector Morse) have found a new life as TV heroes.

TV writers

Many of England's best playwrights started by writing for television when they were young, and some still come back to this medium when they wish to write for a bigger audience than they can find in the theatre. Just a few of the names in this large group are **Harold Pinter**, **Tom Stoppard**, **Alan Bennett**, **Denis Potter**, **Alan Bleasdale**, **Hanif Kureishi** and **Stephen Poliakoff**. Although he did write for the theatre, Potter's name, more than any of the others in the list, is associated with television. He produced a body of work which is still talked about and re-broadcast several years after his death. Perhaps his best were a six-part drama, *Pennies from Heaven*; a powerful play about childhood, *Blue Remembered Hills*; and another fascinating drama series, *The Singing Detective.*

Actors

England has a long theatrical tradition; part of this is the training which many actors receive at the top drama training schools, for example RADA (The Royal Academy for Dramatic Art), The Central School of Speech and Drama, or The Bristol Old Vic Theatre School. After training, some actors may hope to find experience in one of the big companies such as The Royal National Theatre or The Royal Shakespeare Company, or in a long-running TV series. Although many top actors are tempted to go and earn more money in Hollywood films, some like to return to the British theatre from time to time in order to meet the challenge that only a live audience can give.

English actors of stage and screen

Some of England's greatest living actors remain in demand not only in Hollywood but also with European film directors. Here is a list of some of England's current top stars, together with the names of their best-known films and an indication of whether they won a Hollywood Oscar or a BAFTA award (the British Academy of Film and Television Arts). By the way, Sean Connery, Anthony Hopkins and Kenneth Branagh are not in the list, as they are from Scotland, Wales and Northern Ireland respectively!

Actor	Films	Oscar or BAFTA?
Michael Caine	*The Ipcress File*	
	Educating Rita	BAFTA
	Hannah and Her Sisters	Oscar
Peter O'Toole	*Lawrence of Arabia*	BAFTA
Jeremy Irons	*Brideshead Revisited* (TV)	

	Reversal of Fortune	Oscar
	The French Lieutenant's Woman	
Emma Thompson	*Howard's End*	Both
	Sense and Sensibility	BAFTA (actress) Oscar (for the script)
Ben Kingsley	*Gandhi*	Both
	Schindler's List	
Judi Dench	*Mrs Brown*	BAFTA
	Shakespeare in Love	Oscar
	James Bond films (as 'M')	
Daniel Day-Lewis	*My Left Foot*	Both
	The Last of the Mohicans	
	In the Name of the Father	
Maggie Smith	*The Prime of Miss Jean Brodie*	Both
	California Suite	Oscar
	Tea with Mussolini	
John Hurt	*The Elephant Man*	BAFTA
	Midnight Express	BAFTA
	Alien	
	Captain Corelli's Mandolin	
Ralph Fiennes	*The English Patient*	
	Schindler's List	BAFTA
	Quiz Show	

There are also many popular actors who have won awards for other performances: for example, Hugh Grant, Kate Winslet, Helen Mirren, Vanessa Redgrave, Albert Finney, Nigel Hawthorne and Alan Bates.

Directors and films

England is also rich in the number of talented film and theatre directors it has, even though the money and opportunity Hollywood offers will draw some away. Two of the currently 'hot' film directors – Sam Mendes (director of the Oscar-winning *American Beauty*) and Stephen Daldry (*Billy Elliot*) – are known chiefly as men of the theatre, but achieved great success with their first films. So did Nicholas Hytner, with the film of *The Madness of King George*, but in 2001 he was appointed as the new head of the Royal National Theatre, and so will be limiting himself to the theatre for the next few years at least.

As the film industry within England has become smaller, many of our leading film directors have found more opportunities available in Hollywood, as can be seen from the following list. Nevertheless, many films are still made in England since film companies and directors appreciate the experience and high quality of the technical work done by English studios and technicians.

English directors		
Director		**Best-known films**
Richard Attenborough	b. 1923	*Gandhi, Chaplin, Cry Freedom, Shadowlands*
Stephen Frears	b. 1931	*My Beautiful Laundrette, Dangerous Liaisons*
Ken Loach	b. 1936	*Kes, Riff-Raff, Raining Stones, Land and Freedom, My Name is Joe*
Ridley Scott	b. 1939	*Alien, Blade Runner, Thelma and Louise, Gladiator*
Mike Leigh	b. 1934	*High Hopes, Life is Sweet, Naked, Secrets and Lies*
Mike Newell	b. 1943	*Four Weddings and a Funeral*
Alan Parker	b. 1944	*Bugsy Malone, Midnight Express, Fame, The Commitments, Evita*
Anthony Minghella	b. 1954	*Truly Madly Deeply, The English Patient, The Talented Mr Ripley*

Danny Boyle	b. 1956	*Shallow Grave, Trainspotting, The Beach*
Peter Cattaneo	b. 1964	*The Full Monty*
Guy Ritchie	b. 1968	*Lock Stock and Two Smoking Barrels, Snatch*

Advertising

Many of the directors in the above list started work, and still work from time to time, in advertising. Such creative people have helped give British advertising a strong reputation. Visitors to England are often impressed by the quality of the advertisements shown on TV or featured in magazines. These often show English wit, irony and design at their best. After all, more planning per second goes into an advertisement and more money per second is spent on (and made from) an advert than on any other artistic activity. So it is perhaps not surprising that a lot of them are very good. Well-known actors (eg Anthony Hopkins for Barclays Bank) or sports personalities (eg Gary Lineker for Walker's crisps) are often used to promote the products.

In 2000, *The Sunday Times* and Channel 4 Television asked people to name the best television advertisements of all time. The clear winner was a 60-second advert for Guinness beer made in 1999 by Jonathan Glazer. It featured horses and surfers, and was described by a journalist as 'the most beautiful and powerful piece of film on our screens'. Glazer began by making pop videos, and in 2001 made his first feature film, *Sexy Beast*. Other TV adverts in the top ten of all time were for Tango orange drink, Boddington's beer, Hamlet cigars and Walker's crisps. The most important English agencies in this field are Saatchi & Saatchi, Bartle Bogle Hegarty and Abbott Mead Vickers.

Food and drink

Traditionally, food was a topic in which the English did not take great interest; certainly no visitor used to expect good food in

England. But the last ten or fifteen years have seen a great change. This is partly due to the greater expectations that English people now have after taking holidays in other countries where food is more varied and better prepared. Although every English town has its fast food centres, good food is not to be found there. Instead, go to pubs, sandwich bars and restaurants for interesting, tasty or exotic dishes. There are many foreign chefs in England, it is true. However, there are now a lot of well-trained English chefs who have had experience abroad, and who are running their own restaurants. Food and wine are now talked about more than ever: as testified by the explosion of TV programmes on these topics.

Cookery writers

Before the current interest in food, England had some excellent cookery writers. Elizabeth David was the first to open English eyes to the pleasures of Mediterranean food, and Jane Grigson's books on traditional English cooking were very popular. However, this was nothing compared with the current demand for cookery books. **Delia Smith** is the first TV chef to have become a national celebrity. Her first name is even listed in new dictionaries as a word by itself, as in *to do a Delia* (meal) or *to make a Delia* (recipe)! Her cookery books, such as *The Complete Illustrated Cookery Course* or *One is Fun*, and her TV programmes have been hugely popular. Where she leads, many now follow. All the TV channels have programmes devoted to cookery, featuring 'celebrity chefs' such as Jamie Oliver (*The Naked Chef*), Gary Rhodes, Nigella Lawson, Rick Stein (a seafood expert) and Keith Floyd. There are also experts resident in England who tell us all about the tastes of Middle Eastern food (Claudia Roden) and Chinese cooking (Ken Lo).

English wine

The English are now drinking more wine at home or in restaurants than ever before. Although it is mainly foreign wine (Australian, French, Chilean, and so on) that is drunk, there are many English vineyards trying to establish their white wines on the market. After all, when the Romans ruled England two thousand years ago, they produced a lot of wine, so why shouldn't we? There are two problems: firstly, most supermarkets do not stock much English wine, as they feel their customers prefer that of better-known producers; secondly, English wine, because of higher tax and labour costs, ends up more expensive than its rivals. Can English creativity find a way round this problem?

Contrary to what you might expect fish 'n' chips is NOT the most popular food of the English. That award now goes to – curry! A report in 2001 announced that this Indian dish (but produced in a way to please English tastes) had taken over the top spot. The rising cost of fish in England has probably reduced its popularity. So perhaps curry 'n' chips will become the dish of the new millennium...

GLOSSARY

controversy important topic that people strongly disagree about

cosmetics make-up for the face or body

eccentric strange or unusual, sometimes in an amusing way

espionage spying, or secret discovery of the political or military secrets of another country

fan-club organization for keen supporters or admirers of someone or something

greenhouse building made of glass, for growing plants that need warmth

guru leader or expert on a particular subject

impartiality quality of not showing support for any person or group more than another

label company which produces goods for sale

locomotive railway engine that pulls a train

longitude the position to the east or west of an imaginary line on the Earth's surface

propellors two or more blades which turn at high speed, causing a ship or plane to move

quarry large man-made hole in the ground from which stones, sand, etc are dug out for use in building

rococo very decorated and detailed eighteenth-century European style of art, furniture, etc

slogan short, easily-remembered phrase, often used in advertising

supersonic travelling faster than the speed of sound

surfers people who ride sea waves on specially-made boards

surreal strange; more like a dream than reality

suspension (bridge) supported by strong steel ropes hung from a tower at each end

terrestrial of TV channels which are broadcast from stations on the ground (unlike satellite TV)

trams electric, passenger-carrying vehicles that run along rails in towns

Taking it further

Suggested reading

Childs, Peter, *Encyclopedia of Contemporary British Culture*,
   Routledge, 1999
Hillier, Bevis and McIntyre, Kate, *The Style of the Century*, Herbert
   Press, 1998   Focuses on the style and look of British inventions
New Theatre   Quarterly journal
Patten, Marguerite, *A Century of British Cooking*, Grub Street, 2001
Sight and Sound   The British Film Institute's magazine
Street, Sarah, *British National Cinema*, Routledge, 1997
Strong, Roy, *The Spirit of Britain*, Pimlico, 2000   About
   Britain's cultural achievement
Yapp, Nick (ed), *The British Millennium*, Konemann UK Ltd, 2000

Websites

Design and engineering

http://www.enchantedlearning.com   For inventors and
   inventions from 1400 to 2000
http://www.itv-f1.com   For information on Formula One motor-
   racing
http://www.morgan-motor.co.uk
http://www.designmuseum.org
http://www.britishdesign.co.uk   Contains information about the
   British design awards

Media

http://www.widemedia.com   For news about exhibitions taking
   place in England
http://www.bfi.org.uk   The British Film Institute's website
http://www.bbc.co.uk   With links to all the BBC's sites
http://www.artsonline.com
http://www.mediazoo.co.uk   For up-to-date news and ideas about
   British media
http://www.artsworld.com
http://www.artsjournal.com   Daily information on arts and culture
http://www.bafta.org   For news of the BAFTA awards

Cookery

All of the chefs mentioned in the chapter have their own books and their own websites! For a general summary of the best of English food, try Marguerite Patten's book (details above).

Fashion

All of the leading designers have their own websites; one informative general site is **http://www.fashionwindows.com**

General

http://www.english-heritage.org.uk For information on England's heritage sites
http://www.information-britain.co.uk A useful site for tourists

Museums

If you come to England, then try to visit some of the wonderful museums in London or other cities. Many have been redesigned and now include computerized displays and interactive videos. Here are a few suggestions (they all have websites):

London: Tate Britain, Tate Modern, The British Museum, Somerset House, The Natural History Museum, The Science Museum, The Victoria and Albert Museum, The Imperial War Museum, The Theatre Museum, Museum of the Moving Image, Madame Tussaud's Wax Museum.

Elsewhere: The Jorvik Viking Centre, The National Railway Museum, and The Museum of Automata (all in York); The National Museum of Photography, Film and Television (Bradford); The National Motorcycle Museum (Solihull), The National Motor Museum (Beaulieu); The Ironbridge Gorge Museum (Shropshire).

http://www.nmsi.ac.uk is a useful general site (for various English museums)

8 | POLITICAL STRUCTURES AND INSTITUTIONS

The UK is one political entity which includes England, Scotland, Wales and Northern Ireland and is ruled by Parliament in London. Politics in England have been closely entangled with those of Scotland, Wales and Northern Ireland for so long that it is difficult to discuss one country completely separately from the others. The principal focus in this chapter is England but the discussion will cover issues relevant to the whole of the UK.

The government

The Labour Party has been in government since it won the general election in May 1997. Its politics are broadly left of centre. Until the election, there had been eighteen years of rule by a very right of centre Conservative Party, first led by Margaret Thatcher (1979–1990), and then by John Major (1990–1997). When Labour was re-elected to power in the June 2001 general election it was a landslide victory – in fact, the biggest ever achieved by a party in government.

The constitution

A constitution is the system of laws which describes people's rights, such as the right to freedom of speech. Unlike most countries, the UK does not have a written constitution contained in any one single document. It has evolved over the centuries and is to be found in statutes (laws created in Parliament), common law (laws based upon decisions made in the courts) and in conventions (accepted ways of doing things). For example, the prime minister (also known as the PM) is the most powerful person in the country but there are no laws about who becomes PM. It is accepted that this will be the leader of the largest party in the House of Commons (see page 155). The current PM is Tony Blair, leader of the Labour Party.

The European dimension

The European Union (EU) now has a role to play in the way the country is governed. Where UK and EU laws conflict, in cases concerning the environment, health and safety at work, industrial and equal opportunity policies, it is the EU laws which take precedence. One example is the UK law concerning sex discrimination in the workplace. The EU decided that the UK 1975 Sex Discrimination Act did not meet European standards and that the UK government had to make the legislation more favourable to women seeking equal pay. The government had to change the law so that a woman seeking equal pay could compare herself with a man doing work of similar value, as opposed to the previous situation where she could only compare herself to a man who is doing exactly the same work. The European dimension is thus having a real effect upon people's lives.

The European dimension is also having a profound impact upon party politics. Since the 1990s, the Conservative Party in particular has been seriously divided over attitudes to Europe. Generally speaking, the 'Thatcherites' have been against further integration into Europe arguing that it would be a surrender of national sovereignty. The pro-Europe section of the party feels that, as we now live in a global marketplace, we need to be at the heart of Europe and to be a central part of the European Union in order to compete with the American and Asian economies.

The monarchy

The UK is a constitutional and hereditary monarchy. Queen Elizabeth II is the current monarch and head of state. In 2002 she celebrated her 'golden jubilee' – fifty years as Queen – marked by an extra public holiday in June of that year. In theory, the monarch has enormous power, for example to dissolve Parliament, to appoint a new prime minister and to declare war; all new laws must receive the monarch's assent. In practice, the responsibilities of government are carried out by 'her' ministers and the monarch's role is ceremonial. The Queen's power rests largely in the influence she has, for example through the weekly meetings with the prime minister or in public speeches. All real power is in the House of Commons in Parliament. The monarch does not vote in elections. By convention, she or he does not become involved in party politics and is expected to be completely impartial. The present Queen's relationship with the various prime ministers over the last fifty years has, with one notable exception, been very good. It is no secret that the Queen and Margaret Thatcher disagreed and were not close.

The future of the monarchy

Feelings about the continued existence of the monarchy are not passionate. There is not a strong republican movement in English politics. Some people, probably the majority, would like to keep the monarchy; others would not, but nobody gets too excited about the issue. Rather the debate is about what should be the role of the Royal Family. Should we continue to support them financially? Public money (called 'the civil list') is given to the Royal Family to cover the costs of official duties, for example, in 2000 £16.4 million was spent on the royal palaces and on media and information services. Newspapers and television regularly publish information about how much individual royals receive and what duties they perform. In a survey by *The Guardian* newspaper just one in ten people thought the Royal Family was good value for money. On the other hand, it is argued that the monarchy attracts tourists and therefore brings a lot of money into the country.

Undoubtedly, the Royal Family's public image has suffered in recent times – with the exception of the Queen and the late Queen Mother who remain popular figures. Since the Victorian era and until recently, the Royal Family presented themselves as the ideal of happy family life, but the marital problems and misadventures of the princes and their wives have damaged the monarchy's reputation. At the time of Princess Diana's death, the Windsors, ie the Royal Family, were portrayed in the media as cold and unsympathetic characters. This view was shared by many of the general public. As a result, for the first time ever, the Queen hired a team of public relations advisors. The media and the public are not as deferential towards the monarchy as they used to be. We live in an age of celebrity and the royals are treated (or mistreated) as just another celebrity family, pursued by the paparazzi and appearing in 'celebrity gossip' magazines like *Hello* and *OK*.

As well as being the UK head of state, the Queen is head of state in fifteen other commonwealth countries (see also Chapter Twelve). It is probable that many of these will loosen or even break this connection with the mother country as integration with neighbouring states develops. Australia and New Zealand will quite possibly become republics in the near future. This will further decrease the importance of the monarchy.

The Houses of Parliament

The most famous symbol of England is Parliament. It is one long building which consists of 'Big Ben' (the clock tower), the House of Commons and, at the other end, the House of Lords. Constitutional changes in 1911 and 1949 have limited the power of the Lords to revising and checking laws that are proposed in the Commons. Ultimately, the decision-making power is with the Commons, and any criticisms or suggestions from the Lords can be overruled. The Labour Party made reform of the Lords one of its 1997 election policies. It is currently half-way through that reform process. Under the old system, the House of Lords was made up of hereditary members (known as 'hereditary peers') and 'life peers' who were appointed by the government because of a distinguished record in the community, politics, business or the arts. (See page 161.) Some members of the Lords are also judges; they act as the highest court of appeal in England. The leading figures in the Church of England (such as the Archbishop of Canterbury) have seats in the Lords too.

The Houses of Parliament

The most important institution in the country is the House of Commons. It consists of six hundred and fifty-nine members (called Members of Parliament or MPs) who are democratically elected: five hundred and twenty-nine represent people living in England; Wales has forty MPs; Scotland seventy-two and Northern Ireland eighteen. Its powers are unrestricted as there is no written constitution and has therefore been described as 'an elective dictatorship'.

Government ministers

The prime minister (PM) is the key politician. He or she has the power of patronage, that is the power to appoint MPs to more senior jobs in the government and to dismiss them. Having won the election, the PM chooses about one hundred MPs to become government ministers and manage the various government departments. It is also possible, though not common, for a minister to be chosen from the House of Lords. The most important government ministers after the prime minister are the Chancellor of the Exchequer, whose role is to look after economic and financial affairs, the Home Secretary who is concerned with law and order, and the Foreign Secretary who is responsible for foreign policy. Although the PM normally stays in his or her job until the next general election, ministers are usually re-shuffled about every two years. The most senior ministers in the government become members of a committee called the 'cabinet'. The cabinet meets weekly in the PM's home and office, 10 Downing Street (which is very near Parliament) to discuss the key issues affecting government.

The second largest party, which at the moment is the Conservative Party, is known as the 'official Opposition'. Its leader, currently Iain Duncan-Smith, forms his own 'shadow cabinet'.

General election results for the three main political parties (2001)

	Votes	% share of vote	% share of people eligible to vote	MPs elected
Labour	10,724,953	40.7	24.2	412
Conservative	8,357,615	31.7	18.7	166
Liberal Democrat	4,814,321	18.3	10.7	52

(Turnout 59.4%)

Elections

Elections must take place every five years. The PM can decide to call an election before that time if he or she feels it is necessary. In practice, this usually means an election is called when the PM thinks his or her party is likely to win another election. The UK electoral system is often described as the 'first past the post system' – like a horse race in which there is only one winner. Each Member of Parliament represents a 'constituency' – an area with a population of about ninety thousand inhabitants. With a few exceptions, such as people in prison and the monarch, anyone over the age of 18 can vote and anyone over the age of 21 can stand for election as an MP. The candidate who receives more votes than any other single candidate wins the election and becomes the MP for that constituency. Votes for the losing candidates are ignored. The party with the most MPs in the House of Commons forms the government. As a result there is usually one-party government, unlike in other countries where different electoral systems may favour coalition governments.

Under this system, what matters is the number of MPs that a party has in the House of Commons. Some people, especially the Liberal Democrats, feel this is unfair. In the 2001 election, the Liberal Democrats won 18.3 per cent of the votes and gained 52 MPs. However, the Conservative Party won 31.7 per cent of the votes but gained 166 MPs.

Elections to the European Parliament operate under the same rules as those in other member states. Consequently, the electoral system is different to that used in the UK general elections. A proportional voting system is used. In this system the number of seats a party has in the European Parliament reflects the proportion of votes gained in the election. There are six hundred and twenty-six directly elected members of the European Parliament (MEPs) – eighty-seven from the United Kingdom.

European Parliament election results for the three main political parties (1999)

	Members of European Parliament (MEPs)	% of the vote
Conservative	36	35.17
Labour	29	27.55
Liberal Democrat	10	12.44
(Turnout 24%)		

Voter apathy

Voting is not compulsory and the number of people taking part in elections is often low. Only 59 per cent of people eligible to vote in England bothered to vote in the 2001 general election. It was one of the lowest turnouts ever. Labour became the largest party in the

House of Commons and formed a government on the basis of support from only 24.2 per cent of the total number of people eligible to vote. This was despite new schemes to attract voters such as new postal voting rules, and transforming pubs and even fish and chip shops into polling stations. In the British elections for the European Parliament in June 1999, the turnout was only 24 per cent – the lowest of all the countries in the EU!

Part of the explanation for voter apathy may be found in the mistrust of politicians which developed during the Conservative government of the 1990s. In a survey taken in 1974, 40 per cent of people said that 'most of the time' they trusted the government to put the country's interest above those of their own party. By 1991 the figure had fallen to 31 per cent and in 1997 to 22 per cent. There was a short recovery in 1997 after Labour's election victory, but by late 2001 it had dropped to 16 per cent – an all time low (British Social Attitudes Survey, 2001).

Are voters apathetic because politics in England is less interesting today? During the Thatcher era there was a clear division between strong supporters of government policies and equally ardent opponents. Many liked the 'iron lady' and her confrontational style of government. And many hated her and her policies. Tony Blair's Labour Party has moved towards the centre ground in politics, and in doing so has attracted many former Tory supporters. The Conservative Party currently offers weak opposition. Its policies are similar to Labour's and it has deeply divided attitudes to Europe. In any case, Labour has such a huge majority in the House of Commons that it does not need to worry about opposition in Parliament.

Financing politics

Political parties do not receive funds from the state. They are dependent upon private contributions. The Conservative Party receives money from big business as well as from private individuals. The Labour Party receives large donations from the trade unions and individuals too. In the 1990s there was concern about money received by the Conservative Party from donors living overseas, and the rules about donations were altered.

Since February 2001 political parties can only accept money from 'permissible donors' who are people or companies with a base in the UK. There are also limits on what political parties and individuals can spend on their election campaigns. Hence elections in England tend to be much less colourful (and less costly) than in the United States, for example.

Local government

When we talk about politics in England we tend to think about the Houses of Parliament and Westminster, ie about national politics. However, on a day-to-day basis, people in England are much more involved with local government than they are with national government. Most public services, such as schools, roads and the collection of rubbish, are organized at local government level. In the past, local government would employ their own staff to carry out these services. However, in recent times there has been a move towards employing private companies to do the work, especially cleaning and maintenance.

Local government receives finance both from central government and from the Council Tax which is related to the value of a house or a flat. The more expensive the property, the more Council Tax you must pay.

Political institutions at the local level operate in a similar way to those at the national level. Candidates stand for election, usually as members of one of the main political parties. When elected, they become councillors. Meetings and debates take place in the town or county hall. The turnout for local elections is normally very low – often well below 40 per cent, the lowest in Europe in fact. Although some independent candidates are elected, the main political parties dominate local politics. However, voting in local elections does not always reflect the trend at the national parliamentary elections. Although the Conservative Party had a very bad result in the 2001 general election, they did well in the county council elections in the same year. Evidence suggests that some voters were dividing their loyalties between Conservative councillors on the one hand and Labour MPs on the other. The results in 2001 were also particularly disappointing for the Liberal Democrats who traditionally do much better at the local elections and are particularly active and influential in local politics.

Until the year 2000, London was the only capital city in Europe without a directly elected government. Although there were local elections in different parts of the city there was no effective organization responsible for overall control. After the May 2000 elections London became the first city in England to have a directly elected mayor – Ken Livingstone. If this is a success, other large English cities may follow London's example.

Constitutional reform

Reform of the House of Lords

Until very recently, most members of the House of Lords were hereditary peers. One of the Labour Party's election promises was to modernize the Lords. The first of the two stages of their reform process was introduced in 1999. The right of seven hundred and fifty hereditary peers to sit and vote in the Lords was abolished; ninety-two remain temporarily. In the second stage, the remaining hereditary peers will lose their parliamentary rights. The members of a new upper house will be partly elected and partly appointed by the government.

Electoral reform

Many people feel the electoral system in UK general elections is unfair and should be changed to a form of proportional representation. The government commission on electoral reform produced a report in November 1998 which recommended the introduction of 'the alternative vote plus' system. Commentators in newspapers and on TV complained that it is complex and difficult to understand. The government has not moved any further forward on this issue. It is also reported in the media that because there appears to be no straightforward solution and because he has been distracted by more pressing concerns, the prime minister has lost interest. For the time being, electoral reform has been put on the shelf.

Devolution – what about England?

Devolution means the transfer of power from a superior to an inferior political institution. As a result of devolution in the United Kingdom in the late 1990s, Scotland, Wales and Northern Ireland became more independent. Scotland now has its own Parliament in Edinburgh. In Wales there is the Welsh Assembly. A new assembly was also set up in Northern Ireland as a part of the 'Good Friday agreement' to end the hostilities and violence in the region. The power of these regional institutions is limited and ultimate authority still rests with the UK Parliament in London.

There are no plans to establish a separate assembly or Parliament for England and support for such a change is not really significant. In a survey 62 per cent of people thought it was best for England to be governed as it is at the moment. Only 18 per cent wanted England to have its own Parliament. However, the government is considering setting up regional assemblies; England would be divided into eight regions, each with its own elected regional administration. The politics of the regions is likely to become increasingly significant in the future, especially concerning the differences between the poorer north and the wealthier south – often referred to as the north–south divide.

Another recent development has been the establishment of the Greater London Authority (the GLA) and the first directly elected mayor. Ken Livingstone ('Red Ken' as the press used to call him) won the mayoral election with a landslide victory despite strong opposition from his former colleagues in the Labour Party. He has had a few battles with central government, for example about how to finance improvements to the London transport system; he opposed their plan for partial privatization of the tube (London's underground rail system) and has proposed a £5 per day charge for vehicles coming into central London. If London's local government experience is repeated in the proposed regional assemblies, then local politics in England will be stormy but interesting.

Political parties

Since 1945, it has been either the Labour Party or the Conservative Party which has won the general election and formed the government. During that time they have each won eight general elections. In 2001, seventy-eight 'political parties' took part in the general election. The Labour Party, Conservative Party and the Liberal Democratic Party between them accounted for over 90 per cent of the votes.

The Labour Party

The origins of the Labour Party go back to the nineteenth century and are closely connected with the growth of the trade union movement, the emergence of an urban industrial working class and the spread of socialist ideology. After the First World War the Labour Party rapidly developed into the principal opposition to the Conservative Party. Labour has been in government between 1945–1951, 1964–1970, 1974–1979 and since 1997.

Before its 1997 election victory, the Labour Party had been out of government for eighteen years. During that time, under the leadership of Neil Kinnock, John Smith and Tony Blair, its policies moved further towards the centre of politics. Under Tony Blair, the party was renamed 'New Labour'. Its ties with the trade union movement weakened and it promoted less radical economic ideas about the redistribution of wealth. In doing so its appeal widened, especially among the middle classes. Critics complain, however, that it is no longer truly socialist. In the UK elections, its main support is in the metropolitan areas and less wealthy parts of the country, such as the north-east. It also tends to get more support from younger people and the majority of black and Asian voters.

The Conservative Party (also known as the 'Tory Party' or the 'Tories')

The origins of the Conservative Party go back to the eighteenth century. Its policies are right of centre and its supporters are traditionally from business and the wealthier groups in society.

During the 1980s, with Thatcher as leader, it was a confident, united party and victorious in successive elections. During the 1990s it became fractious and disunited, especially over attitudes towards the European Union. Scandals about 'sleaze' and politicians accepting bribes damaged its image. In the 1997 and 2001 general elections it was very heavily defeated. Its leader, William Hague, was not a popular figure and the issues upon which he contested the general election (such as whether Britain should adopt the Euro) were poor choices. The electorate were more interested in how to improve public services like the hospitals, roads and schools. In 2001 it chose a new leader, Iain Duncan-Smith. The current leadership of the Conservative Party has been dismissed as a group of 'has-beens and never-weres managed by never-will-bes' (source: Anthony King, 'Why Britons will turn away from Westminster' in *The World in 2002*, The Economist Newspaper Limited). A harsh criticism. No doubt the party will, in time, recover from these setbacks but at the moment it seems unlikely to win the next general election.

The Liberal Democratic Party (also known as the 'Lib-Dems')

The Liberal Democrats form the third largest party. Traditionally, their politics are somewhere between the Labour and Conservative parties – though, under their last two leaders, the party has been leaning more towards Labour. It was created in the late 1980s as a result of a merger between the Liberal Party and the Social Democratic Party. The Liberal Democrats have always gained a much larger share of the vote than their representation in Parliament would suggest and, not surprisingly, they have been the prime mover in favour of electoral reform. They are pro-Europe and want a more powerful European Union. Traditionally their support has been strongest in south-west England and the party has had a strong presence in local politics. In the 2001 elections they gained their best ever result (fifty-two MPs).

Key political personalities

Tony Blair

Tony Blair is the prime minister and the leader of the Labour Party. He is one of the principal architects responsible for modernizing the Party and making it electable again after the disastrous years of the 1980s. He has been very popular with the electorate, although opinion polls indicate this popularity has decreased from its very high point just after the 1997 election. There are criticisms that his style is too presidential and that he makes too many decisions without properly consulting other ministers. It is said he cares more for his image on the international stage than he does for domestic issues.

Gordon Brown

Gordon Brown is Chancellor of the Exchequer and second in rank to the prime minister. His management of the economy has been skilful and earned him and the Labour Party much credit. He is frequently mentioned as the politician most likely to succeed Tony Blair as leader of the party.

Iain Duncan-Smith

Iain Duncan-Smith became the Conservative Party leader after the disastrous performance of the Tories in the 2001 general election. He is a Eurosceptic right-winger and critics describe him as a dull politician but, more importantly, say that he has no clear idea of how to engineer a Tory recovery. To be fair, it will inevitably take time to establish his presence on the political scene.

Charles Kennedy

As the leader of the Liberal Democrats, Charles Kennedy (a Scot) is an able speaker in Parliament and on television. He is popular with the general public and led his party in their most successful election campaign ever in 2001.

Women in politics

In the 2001 election, one hundred and eighteen women became MPs. This represents 18 per cent of the total number of MPs and is well below the European average figure of 25 per cent for membership of equivalent institutions. There is now a Minister for Women in the government.

Pressure groups

These are organizations which seek to influence government but do not fight elections or seek to become the government. They are an important part of the political process as more people belong to pressure groups than to political parties. There is an enormous range of groups, for example, trade unions, animal rights groups, groups representing business such as the Confederation of British Industry.

The language of politicians

A cliché is a word or expression that is very familiar and has been used so often that it is not effective. We all use them. Examples of common English clichés are *you must be joking* meaning 'what you have just told me is surprising'. Another cliché is *let's face it* which we use when stating a fact that is unpleasant or that we do not really want to admit, for example: *let's face it, nobody tells the truth to the tax authorities*. They are ready-made pieces of language which save us the trouble of thinking for ourselves. Research has been carried out on politicians' favourite clichés. Here are some of them:

> *There is no instant solution*
> *Let me at this stage be absolutely open and honest*
> *It's going to take time*
> *There are no easy answers*
> *Our message is very simple and very clear*
> *The dire situation we inherited from the previous administration...*

Tony Blair's favourite cliché is *we have achieved a great deal, but there is still much to do*. The researcher found that politicians use clichés to avoid answering questions or to give themselves time to think while trying to remember the party line on a particular issue (source: 'Politicians' favourite clichés revealed', Sarah Hall, *The Guardian*, 29 May 2001).

The future of Parliament

- **Devolution**   Are the recent constitutional changes the start of the break up of the UK? Much has been written on the subject by 'the chattering classes' (a disparaging phrase used to describe academics, politicians, writers and intellectuals), for example, *The Death of Britain* by John Redwood (a Conservative politician) and *The Abolition of Britain* by Christopher Hitchens, (a journalist). At the moment the break up of the UK seems very unlikely.

- **Europe**   The growing importance of the European Union over large areas of policy is a subject of much controversy. It divides the political parties as well as the electorate. A referendum will be held to decide whether to abolish the pound sterling as Britain's currency and replace it with the Euro. However, it seems inevitable that the country will move further into the European Union and join the European currency.

- **The monarchy**   The monarchy looks much less secure now than it did even twenty years ago. It will not be abolished but it does seem increasingly irrelevant in modern society. Much work needs to be done by the Royal Family and its public relations advisors to restore its reputation.

- **The media and politics**   In recent years, media coverage of politics has been changing. Newspapers no longer carry detailed reports of parliamentary debates, perhaps because these are now televised. However, with television coverage, attention is sometimes distracted from the subject of the debate by the spectacle of inter-party verbal warfare accompanied by loud heckling from backbenchers. Prime minister's question time, which takes place on Wednesdays, is sufficiently interesting or entertaining to have found a slot on American television.

Journalists complain that political news is increasingly manipulated and distorted by press officers who represent the government and political parties (also called disparagingly 'spin doctors' – because they alter information so that it has a sympathetic viewpoint or 'spin').

GLOSSARY

assent agreement, approval

backbenchers name given to MPs who sit on the back benches in Parliament. These seats are taken by members who do not have any official position in government or in an opposition political party

coalition government involving two or more political parties who agree to work together

colleague somebody you work with

commission group of people, usually with specialist knowledge, formally chosen to investigate a problem, eg electoral reform

Commonwealth association consisting of countries that were once part of the British Empire

court of appeal if a person has been found guilty of a crime, he or she may challenge that decision in a court of appeal

deferential polite and respectful

(to) dissolve Parliament (to) close Parliament

electorate people entitled to vote in an election

Eurosceptic someone who is sceptical (doubtful) about the benefits of Britain being in the European Union

heckling interrupting a public speech with critical remarks or questions

hereditary something that is passed from parent to child

landslide election victory victory that is won by a large number of votes

paparazzi newspaper and magazine photographers who pursue celebrities

party line official view of a political party, eg the party line on transport policy

polling stations places where people vote in elections

privatization government sells an industry, company or service to a private organization

public relations advisors people whose job involves maintaining a good relationship with the media and the general public so that their client is viewed positively

referendum vote by all the people in a country on a specific issue, eg whether or not to join the Euro

right-winger individual whose political beliefs are right-wing, ie conservative and traditionalist

sleaze poor standard of honesty or morality

sovereignty power that a nation has to govern itself

take precedence be considered as most important

Thatcherites people who hold views similar to those of the former prime minister, Margaret Thatcher

trade unions organizations representing workers. They try to improve workers' pay and conditions of employment

turnout the number of people eligible to vote who actually vote in an election

Victorian era period in British history when Victoria was queen (1837–1901)

Westminster area in London which includes the Houses of Parliament and many government offices

Windsor surname of the Royal Family, sometimes described (not very respectfully) as 'the Windsors'; also the name of a town with a famous castle just outside London

Taking it further

Suggested reading

Farman, John, *The Very Bloody History of Britain – without the boring bits*, Red Fox, 2001   An entertaining history of post-1945 Britain

Haseler, Stephen, *The End of the House of Windsor*, I B Taurus, 1993

Morton, Andrew, *Diana: Her True Story – in Her Own Words*, Michael O'Mara, 1998

Pimlott, Ben, *The Queen*, HarperCollins, 2001

Websites

http://www.royal.gov.uk   Information about the British monarchy

http://www.explore.parliament.uk   Explore the workings of UK Parliament

http://www.pm.gov.uk   10 Downing Street's official website

http://www.homeoffice.gov.uk/new_indexs/contitutional.htm   Constitutional issues

http://www.psr.keele.ac.uk   An excellent starting point for detailed information about politics

Places to visit

Visit the Houses of Parliament and watch politicians take part in debates. Every Wednesday the prime minister answers questions.

THE BASICS FOR LIVING

Education

The state education system is normally divided into three sectors: primary (5–11 years), secondary (11–18 years) and tertiary (16+ years).

Primary and secondary schools

Europeans will find much about primary and secondary education that feels, if not exactly the same as in their own country, then fairly familiar. Schooling is compulsory for everyone between the ages of 5 and 16; and between half and two-thirds of all 4-year-olds also attend school. Many pupils (about 65 per cent) continue voluntarily until 18 in order to take higher level exams. The school year usually begins at the start of September and ends in July with breaks for holidays at Christmas and Easter. There are also half-term breaks lasting about one week during each of the three terms: Autumn, Spring and Summer. A term lasts about twelve weeks. State schools, where education is free, take 94 per cent of pupils. Primary and secondary education is the responsibility of local government, although individual schools can 'opt out' of direct local government control.

Schools operate Monday to Friday with no half-days off as in some countries. The day starts at about 9.00 a.m. and finishes between 3.00 and 4.00 p.m. School meals are provided for the mid-day meal break (about 50 minutes) but in most cases have to be paid for. Some pupils prefer to bring their own sandwiches.

Styles of teaching vary but, generally, pupils will have lessons with a teacher at the head of the class and some sessions where they work in small groups. In secondary schools, pupils have different teachers for each subject. In primary school, pupils are taught all the subjects by one class teacher.

Since the 1960s the main method of organizing secondary teaching has been the 'comprehensive' system, that is teaching a range of academically good and weak pupils together in the same school. The majority of children attend their local comprehensive; however, there are significant variations across the country. This is because there are one hundred and fifty-two local education authorities in England and these have an important influence upon the way schools are run in their area. In a few places grammar schools still operate alongside comprehensive schools. In different areas, pupils may attend their comprehensive school between the ages of 11 and 18 and in others they may leave at 16 and go to a sixth form college or to the local community college. There are also middle schools where pupils stay only between the ages of 8 and 14 years.

The National Curriculum

The National Curriculum, which was introduced in the 1990s, outlines what to teach pupils and sets targets describing what pupils should be able to achieve. It is divided into four key stages. English, mathematics, science, physical education, art and design, and information & communications technology (ICT) are taught at all stages. Other subjects, such as history, geography, art and music are only compulsory at stages 3 and 4. 'Citizenship' became a compulsory subject at stages 3 and 4 in 2002.

Key stages of the National Curriculum	
	Ages
Key stage 1	5–7
Key stage 2	7–11
Key stage 3	11–14
Key stage 4	14–16

The National Curriculum was intended to reduce the importance of attending any particular school. Children should receive roughly similar education in whatever school they go to. However, everybody recognizes that schools vary considerably in the quality of the education they provide and parents often agonize over which school to send their children to, some even moving house to a new area to be able to get into a good school. Children in English schools take some kind of official test almost every year. League tables of school test results are published annually so one school's performance can be compared with another's.

The concerns of the current Labour government include raising standards, particularly for the weakest pupils, and meeting the needs of ethnic minorities. The government has encouraged comprehensive schools to develop specialisms in modern foreign languages, the arts, mathematics and science, sport, and technology. These 'specialist schools' receive extra money but in return share resources and provide support in their specialist subject to other local schools. Critics complain that this goes against the comprehensive ideal of mixed ability schooling and re-introduces selection. Another concern of the government has been the shortage of teachers. While there is evidence to show that educational standards in schools are rising, the increasing workload placed upon teachers by educational reforms in recent years has created problems: many have retired early and it has become difficult to attract young people into the profession.

Educational standards

Since 1993 OFSTED (the Office for Standards in Education in England) has carried out inspections of schools at least once every six years. It is unpopular with teachers who generally view OFSTED inspections as heavy-handed, bureaucratic and over-critical. However, OFSTED argues that it has raised standards of teaching. Many parents look at OFSTED reports when deciding which school to send their child to.

Information technology

Today information technology (IT) has a key role in the curriculum. In primary schools there is one computer for every thirteen pupils and in secondary schools one computer for every eight children; 96 per cent of primary and 99 per cent of secondary schools are connected to the Internet.

Religious education

State schools are obliged to provide religious education and to have a daily act of worship. While this means Christianity for the majority, schools also give instruction in the other main religions. However, parents can arrange for their child to be excluded from religious education lessons if they wish.

Public tests: SATs, GCSEs, AS and A levels

School children in England are probably the most examined in the world. They have some kind of official test practically every year from the age of 5 until 18 years. Some tests are more important than others for their future. They are tested on the core subjects, English, mathematics and science at ages 7, 11 and 14. These are Standard Attainment Tests (SATs). The results are then measured against the National Curriculum scale: the typical 7-year-old should achieve level 2, a typical 11-year-old should achieve level 4 and so on. At age 16 pupils usually sit their GCSE exams (General Certificate of Secondary Education). Normally GCSE courses last two years (ages 14–16). After this, many pupils stay on at school for further study. Advanced ('A') level exams are normally taken at age 18. Recently, the government made changes to the A level system in an attempt to broaden the range of subjects studied. In September 2000 the General Certificate of Education A/S (Advanced Subsidiary) level exams were introduced: pupils study four or five subjects for the first year then choose three of these to continue studying up to A level for the second year. Pupils who prefer vocational studies – or want to mix academic and work-related courses – can take 'vocational A levels', for example, Business Information Technology, Travel and Tourism. It is also possible to take a 'key skills' qualification which focuses on the day-to-day skills needed in the workplace, such as information technology and communication skills.

The GCSE and A level exams are not produced by the state but by three independent organizations, called examining boards. Although the syllabuses must receive approval from the government, the exam boards are able to create a variety of different exams. This means that studying, for example A level history, with one exam board may be very different from studying it with another. Schools choose whichever exam board and syllabus they prefer and if they decide they do not like a particular syllabus or exam board they can change. Although most people take their GCSEs and A levels at 16 and 18, it is possible to take them at any age. Indeed many people who have failed exams at school return to studying in later years, perhaps attending an evening class at the local further education college while working during the day.

Teachers

In recent years, teachers have become increasingly demoralized and dissatisfied. Their workload has grown; there have been frequent changes to syllabus requirements; and they have borne the brunt of blame for any poor exam results. Because of these pressures, recruitment to the profession has dropped – applications for primary teacher training fell by about one-third in 1998.

The independent sector

In England about 6 per cent of school children attend independent sector schools. These schools receive no funds from the state and are financed by fees paid by parents. For historical reasons, some schools in the independent sector are called 'private schools' or 'public schools'. In this context, 'public' and 'private' mean the same thing. The most well known are a small group of about twenty public schools which provide a privileged education for their pupils and have produced a large proportion of the country's past and present elite – famous and successful politicians, civil servants and business people.

Pupils at public schools attend either as boarders, who live on the school premises, or as day pupils. Fees can be very expensive. Eton College, attended by Princes William and Harry, is perhaps the most famous public school. It charged £17,604 per year for boarders in 2001. However, most children (86 per cent) at independent schools are day pupils. The average fee for day pupils in 2001 was just over £6000 a year. Not something that many people in England could afford when you appreciate that the average gross (ie before tax) salary is £21,351. Is private education worth it? Well, class sizes are smaller: on average ten pupils per class compared with 20.3 pupils in state schools (source: 1999

DfEE – primary and secondary figures combined). Also, GCSE exam results are better. Over 80 per cent of 15-year-olds at private schools gained five or more GCSE grades A–C in 1999 compared to the national average of 46 per cent. Perhaps it is not surprising that many independent schools are over-subscribed.

Further education

About 30 per cent of pupils leave school at 16 and look for a job. Many of these will probably become involved in training at work or vocational training (eg a car mechanic's course) at the local Further Education College. FE Colleges also provide GCSE and A level courses for those aged 16+ who do not want to continue studying at school because they prefer a more adult atmosphere or because their school does not teach the subjects they want to study. The FE College is where people might also attend evening recreational classes in subjects such as pottery or judo.

Higher education

English universities have a high degree of independence. There is no automatic right of entry to a university; the university decides who to accept. In practice A level exam results are the main criterion and universities will normally specify the grades required. The more prestigious the university and the more popular the course, the higher the grades. Traditionally, it has been difficult to get to university and competition for places, particularly at the institutions with a good reputation like Oxford, Cambridge or the London School of Economics, is intense.

However, in the 1990s the number of universities increased and the numbers of students continuing education after 16 steadily grew: in the late 1970s less than 10 per cent of 18–21-year-olds were in some form of higher education, whereas in 2001 the figure was 30 per cent. The government target is for 50 per cent of children leaving school to go to university by 2005. Consequently, the university system is changing in order to cater for the masses instead of for an elite minority. All universities have felt a strain on their resources and complain about a lack of funds for expansion to meet the government's targets and the problem of maintaining good standards of education.

The daily life of a university student involves a series of lectures and tutorials, with free time each day when they are expected to work independently on their studies. In the past, students received more personal attention from teaching staff. The vast majority of university students complete their studies successfully, the drop-out rate from university is low by comparison with other countries. A report published by the government showed that undergraduates spend 3.5 years at university which is significantly less than in Europe where the figure is 5.1 years. The difference is accounted for by the fact that students in the rest of Europe stay longer than the minimum time required to complete their studies whereas students in England tend to leave as soon as possible. However, it is quite likely that the situation will become increasingly similar to other European countries as a result of the current reforms to the English university system.

Student finances

University tuition fees are related to income and ability to pay. Students under the age of 21 are assessed on the basis of their parents' income. Those over the age of 21 are 'mature' students and assessed independently. Those on low incomes do not pay any fees – in fact, more than half of all students do not pay any fees. The maximum fee in 2001–2 was £1050 per year.

To meet the costs of tuition fees and living expenses, students can take out a loan. The maximum in 2001–2 was £4590 per year. Many students now take part-time jobs to earn money to help with the costs of food and accommodation.

Traditionally students left home at 18 and went away to a university in another part of the country. Increasingly, as in other European countries, they are going to universities near home in order to minimize costs. Tuition fees are a recent innovation and have caused much resentment. There are some signs that fees are deterring students from poorer backgrounds from applying for higher education. The government has promised to review the situation in England.

Degrees: Bachelors, Masters and Doctors

At university, students (undergraduates) normally study for three or four years full-time, and on successful completion of their course obtain a qualification which is called a degree. They are then known as graduates and are entitled to use the letters BA (Bachelor of Arts) or BSc (Bachelor of Science) after their name. Degrees are either an 'honours' degree (and most are) or a 'pass' degree. Honours degrees are awarded in three classes.

The Master's degree is the name for a higher degree qualification. Students for this degree normally take one year of full-time study, or longer if part-time, and upon successful completion they are entitled to use the letters MA (Master of Arts) or MSc (Master of Science) after their name.

The Doctorate (which confers the title Doctor of Philosophy, PhD) is the highest academic qualification. For this students must spend a minimum of three years full-time study producing an academic thesis. However, it often takes a lot longer than that to achieve this qualification as the majority of students at this level will have a full- or part-time job at the same time.

Overseas students in England

Many students from other countries come to study in England. Schools in the independent sector provide education at primary and secondary level for a large number of foreign pupils. The EU's Socrates-Erasmus programme provides grants for university students from the EU, Central and Eastern Europe and a number of other states. Study periods last three to twelve months and include the whole range of academic subjects.

Lifelong learning

Traditionally we have viewed education as a child/teenage/young adult experience. However, with changing work patterns, greater job mobility and greater retraining needs, there is a move towards lifelong learning undertaken either as courses in colleges and universities or more informally at home (perhaps via the Open University) or in the workplace with the aid of IT. There is even a minister for lifelong learning in the government.

Housing

Home ownership

The idea of home ownership appeals very much to the English character. Most people would like to own their home but in England it is a national obsession. English people value their privacy ('An Englishman's home is his castle' is a well-known saying) as well as the degree of financial independence that home ownership represents.

Figures for house price movements are published monthly and make headline news in the national media. Even people who do not own a house or are not even thinking of buying a property are interested in house prices which are a regular topic of conversation in the pub and at dinner tables. Home ownership increased considerably during the twentieth century – in 2000, 69 per cent of homes were owned by people who live in them compared with only 10 per cent in 1900.

Purchasing a house or flat

Nearly everybody buys their home with a loan (mortgage) from the bank or a building society. Typically, you can borrow about two and a half times the value of your annual salary. These loans are usually repaid over a twenty to twenty-five year period. In 2002 the average first-time buyer was spending 28 per cent of their income on monthly mortgage payments. Of course this proportion is liable to change, as mortgage payments are usually linked to general interest rate movements. In 1990, for example, mortgage payments accounted for 60 per cent of a first-time buyer's monthly income! Many owners will sell their property and purchase a more expensive home long before the twenty to twenty-five years are reached. So, although owning a property is highly desired, many people do not have a strong attachment to a particular house or flat. In the last two decades, buying and selling homes has become a way of increasing wealth. First-time buyers would purchase a cheap property, perhaps one that required a lot of building work and refurbishment that they could tackle themselves. As the value of housing steadily increased (house prices rose by 11.3 per cent in England during the period 1999–2000 whereas the rate of inflation was only 2.1 per cent), buyers would sell their first house a few years later and buy a more expensive property, and so on.

It is possible for buyers to deal directly with sellers but most people use estate agents who have premises on every high street. They charge between 1 and 2.5 per cent of the cost of the house for finding a purchaser and are generally thought to be grossly overpaid for what they do. If you are at a party and mention that you work as an estate agent you can expect a good-natured groan in response from the other guests!

Renting

In the 1950s and 1960s there were so many instances of bad landlords exploiting tenants that legislation restricting the behaviour of landlords and protecting tenants' rights was introduced. However, the resulting legislation created difficulties for all landlords. Evicting tenants, for example for non-payment of rent, became costly and time-consuming. Consequently, the number of properties for rent declined. More recently, legislation has been relaxed and more property has become available for rent. About 10 per cent of homes are now rented from private landlords.

Council accommodation and housing associations

After the Second World War there was a large increase in subsidized accommodation provided by local government ('council houses' or 'council flats'). However, during the 1980s Mrs Thatcher wanted to create a 'home-owning democracy' by selling off these properties to tenants at vastly reduced prices – as much as 50 per cent for some tenants. No doubt this was meant to encourage purchasers to vote Conservative. These houses were never replaced so the number of properties available to the local authorities was severely diminished. The proportion of all households using council accommodation gradually declined from 34 per cent in 1981 to 14 per cent in 2002.

A small amount of rented accommodation (6 per cent) is provided by the Registered Social Landlords (some of which are also known as 'Housing Associations'). They are the major providers of new subsidized homes for those in housing need. Unlike other private landlords, for whom letting out property is simply a way to make money, their purpose is to help people find a home.

Homelessness

The problem of homelessness is evident on the streets of many English cities, especially London. The doorways of many of London's most elegant shops are used as sleeping areas every night. The problem is in part the result of unemployment, the selling of council homes in the 1980s without the rebuilding of any new ones, and changes to the way the benefit system (the social welfare system) operates. In part too, it is the sad result of domestic violence, the start of mental illness and physical and sexual abuse – all of which account for much of youth homelessness. Local government authorities are obliged to provide accommodation to those who meet the criteria of a 'priority need': pregnant women, families with children, the elderly or disabled and those homeless because of an emergency. Those who do not fall into these categories 'sleep rough', ie on the streets.

The future

There has been a major increase in the number of people who through choice, family breakdown or other circumstances are living on their own. In 1971, less than one-fifth of homes were single-person households; twenty years later this had risen to a quarter of homes. Half of the people living alone are over pensionable age; and a large number are on their own because of divorce, or are young people no longer living with their families. Whereas, thirty years ago, many young people still lived with their parents until marriage, nowadays, with the trend for later marriage, more and more young people live independently. Because of all these changes it is estimated that about 5 million new homes will have to be built in the next twenty years.

The National Health Service (NHS)

The National Health Service, which was established in 1948, provides (almost) free health care to all. The finance comes mostly from general taxation (81 per cent), plus some from national insurance contributions (12 per cent) – paid by both employee and employer – and 7 per cent from other charges. Use of the NHS is largely free but certain things have to be paid for, for example eye tests, dental treatment and drug prescription charges. When you visit your local doctor or hospital you have to pay only for the medicines – prescription charges were £6.10 per item in 2002. However, certain groups (the over-60s, children, pregnant women, people with certain illnesses and low income groups) are exempt from charges; in 1995, 85 per cent of items ordered on prescription were provided free. If you need to stay in hospital, there is no charge for treatment or medicines.

NHS staff

With about 1 million employees in England, the NHS is one of the world's biggest employers. More than three-quarters of its employees are female. Doctors and dentists are technically self-employed. Pharmacists and opticians are either self-employed or work as employees of an independent business. They are paid by the NHS to provide health services to the public.

When you are ill, and it is not an emergency, you go first to see your local doctor, also called the GP or general practitioner. If necessary, the GP will then refer you to hospital to see a consultant for more specialized treatment.

Crisis in the NHS

The newspapers often use the word 'crisis' about the state of the NHS and regularly run stories about patients being kept on trolleys for hours because of a lack of hospital beds. Although the media are prone to exaggeration, there is no doubt that much needs to be improved. The state of the NHS is at the top of the political agenda and, as usual, the politicians are blaming each other for the problems. Waiting lists for treatment can be very long and there is a serious shortage of doctors and nurses. Poor pay and low morale, together with heavy workloads (caused by the staffing shortages) and other factors have made it difficult to recruit new staff. Thousands of foreign nurses, including many from Spain, China, Australia, New Zealand, South Africa and the Philippines, are being recruited.

Rising expectations and increased demand have placed a great strain on the health services and the NHS is struggling to cope. The

NHS was once the envy of the world and a source of national pride. That boast now seems hard to believe. In comparison with other countries, it often does rather badly. In the latest World Health Organization league table of health systems (2000), the NHS is eighteenth in terms of overall performance – the French came first. A UK government report (the Wanless Report, published in December 2001) concluded that 'we are not keeping up with the quality of service routinely provided in many other countries ... such as ... France, Germany, the Netherlands, Sweden, Australia, Canada and New Zealand'. This was due to 'a combination of cumulative under-investment over the last thirty years' and ineffective 'organizational arrangements'. It revealed that in the UK:

- Cancer survival rates were lower than in the other seven countries investigated.
- Waiting times were longer and more patients reported difficulties seeing a specialist.
- There were fewer doctors and nurses per head of population.
- Women had the shortest life expectancy.
- More children died in the first year of life than in any of the other seven countries except New Zealand.

Reform

The Conservative government (1979–1997) tried to reform the NHS by introducing a more business-like structure. Many hospitals became 'NHS Trusts', able to control their own finances. However, as in any business when times were not good there were cut-backs in services which provoked much anger among the general public. The Labour government which came to power in 1997 is attempting to modify this structure.

The government has a grand ten-year plan to revitalize the health sector and bring it up to European standards. In the shorter term, the NHS plan has these targets to achieve by 2004:

- To increase the number of doctors by 20 per cent and nurses by 10 per cent.
- To enable patients to see a doctor within 48 hours.
- To cut waiting time in hospital accident and emergency departments to 75 minutes on average (by 2005).

- To cut the waiting time for routine outpatient appointments from six to three months.
- To cut the maximum waiting time for inpatient treatment from eighteen to six months.

The government has pledged to increase spending to the level of other European governments. The extra money will be used to increase wages for staff, to recruit new staff and to improve hospital facilities.

NHS Direct

In 1998 the government set up a telephone helpline and Internet advice service (**http://www.nhs.direct.nhs.uk**) which receives around 5 million 'hits' a month. The intention is to expand this and make it a primary point of access to the NHS. It is hoped that greater use of this service will reduce pressure on GPs' surgeries.

Having a baby

Today, nearly all babies are born in hospital – only 2 per cent of births take place at home. Care is provided both before and after the birth by the midwife and/or the mother's GP. During the pregnancy, and for the first year of the baby's life, a woman receives free prescriptions and free dental care.

Care of the elderly

Like other developed economies, England has an ageing population, and government figures suggest that residential and nursing home places will have to increase by 65 per cent over the next thirty years to keep pace with demand. How to finance residential care is a much discussed topic. Currently, if a person has no, or very little, money the state will cover the costs of care. However, if they have assets exceeding £18,500, such as savings or a house that can be sold, they receive no help from the state. Many elderly people have to sell their house when they move into a nursing home. One estimate is that about forty thousand houses a year are sold to pay for residential and nursing home fees.

Food and exercise

Eating habits have been changing over the last twenty years. The British are eating less red meat (for example, beef and lamb) and more fresh fruit. But, on the other hand, they consume fewer fresh green vegetables than in the 1970s. And of course the use of convenience foods (frozen and ready meals) has increased. This is one factor behind the alarming increase in weight problems. Today, 21 per cent of men over 16, and 19 per cent of women are overweight, compared with 6 per cent and 8 per cent twenty years ago. The government is trying to promote healthier diet awareness by providing fresh fruit in schools in selected areas – by 2004 every child in nursery school and infant school (4–6 years) will be given a free piece of fruit every day they attend school.

Smoking, drinking and drugs

Although the trend has been one of steady decline, about 29 per cent of men and 25 per cent of women smoke cigarettes regularly. Smoking is most popular among people in their twenties and early thirties and those in manual occupations. It is also the biggest single cause of death from cancer and is banned in most public buildings; restaurants usually separate smoking and non-smoking areas. As far as drinking patterns are concerned, there has been a general increase in alcohol consumption, especially among young women.

The most frequently used illegal drug among young people is cannabis. Government sources indicate that it had been used by more than 25 per cent of young (16–24-year-old) people in 1998.

Private healthcare

In recent years this sector has been growing, no doubt as a response to worries about the quality of services in the public sector. However, it is still small in comparison with the NHS. In some aspects of healthcare the private sector is particularly important. For example, it provides most of the residential care for the elderly and the physically disabled. It also provides a large proportion of mental health hospital facilities. There are two hundred and thirty private independent hospitals, most of them run by three organisations: BUPA, General Healthcare Group and Nuffield Hospitals. NHS hospitals are also able to raise money by taking some private patients. The NHS has about three thousand beds available to private patients and so it is also one of the biggest providers of private medicine. A substantial proportion of these are foreign fee-paying patients. The main advantage of private healthcare is not that the treatment is better but that it happens more quickly. The following story, taken from *The Guardian* newspaper, is typical. Mr Christopher Denne was diagnosed with cancer and referred by his GP to hospital. The hospital said that because it was so busy Mr Denne faced an eight-week wait. However, the patient was told that the NHS equipment needed to carry out his treatment was reserved for private patients for a certain period each day but was often unused. Mr Denne paid £180 to have the treatment done within three days. 'It was the same (treatment), in the same hospital, with the same people. It amazed me,' Mr Denne said.

Private medical insurance accounts for 70 per cent of the finance for private healthcare. About 20 per cent comes from direct payments by patients and 5 per cent is from the NHS for services provided on its behalf.

The Labour government is pursuing closer links with the private sector. It sees an opportunity to reduce waiting lists, (particularly for non-urgent operations such as hips and knees) as private hospitals usually use just over half of their hospital beds at any one time whereas in NHS hospitals the beds are always in use. This represents a substantial change in attitude since traditionally Labour politicians had been suspicious and even hostile towards the private sector. Trade unions complain that this is the beginning of the privatization of the NHS. The Labour Government's response is 'We are a monopoly funder of healthcare. We do not have to be a monopoly provider.'

Transport

Guide books to England will tell you that transport is, on the whole, good but expensive. And although it is true that travelling around the country as a tourist is not a problem, the public transport system is not as efficient as it should be or as reliable as it used to be. Everybody in England complains about public transport these days and, like the National Health Service and education, it is at the top of the political agenda.

Problems – delays, cancellations and higher fares

The first large-scale government report comparing British and other European public transport systems (published by the Commission for Integrated Transport, November 2001) concluded that British public transport was the worst in Europe!

- The average commuter spends 46 minutes a day travelling – compared to just 23 minutes in Italy.
- People spend more time in traffic jams than in any other country in the European Union.
- People pay more money for their transport than in any other country in the European Union – a public transport journey in the Netherlands is one-third what it would cost in England.
- Fares are subsidized less in the UK than in any other European country.
- Comparatively high costs of travel have encouraged high levels of car use. About half of all households have one car, and the number with two or more cars continues to increase (from 19 per cent in 1990 to 22 per cent in 2000).

Inter-city public transport

Long-distance buses are the cheapest but slowest means of getting around the country. The rail network is extensive and inter-city trains are fast and can be the most pleasant way to travel. Long-distance trains offer seats in first and standard class carriages. Most people travel standard class; first-class compartments are often largely empty.

Trains

The rail network was privatized during the Conservative government (1979–1997). It is widely accepted that this has not been successful as delays and cancellations are common. There have also been some very serious accidents, for example, the

Hatfield disaster in 2000 in which four people were killed and many were injured. In January 2000, Peter Hain, Government Minister for Europe, declared 'We have the worst railways in Europe.' A chronic lack of investment over a period of thirty years (ie during public, and now private, ownership) means that parts of the infrastructure, for example signalling and rail tracks, are old and in need of replacement. However, demand for train services has been increasing, thus making the problems even worse. More people are travelling by rail than at any time since the 1960s and since privatization in 1997, passengers numbers are up by one-fifth. This is because of cut-price fares, clever marketing and too much traffic on the roads. In October 2000, the government decided that Railtrack, the organization responsible for the tracks upon which the trains run, was not operating on a sound financial basis, and declared it bankrupt. Meanwhile large salaries for top management in the rail companies have alienated and angered the public. The future of the industry is uncertain.

Urban public transport

Buses

As in many other countries, buses are delayed by traffic jams caused by the large number of private cars. Some English cities have introduced special bus lanes giving priority to public transport. In London, they are indicated by a red line along the road. Although there are some late night bus services, most finish at about midnight, which people feel is too early. Another problem is recruiting bus drivers, as the cost of living, especially accommodation, in big city areas like London, is very high. London's famous red double-decker buses (with seating on two levels) are still much in evidence on the roads of the capital. Originally, all buses had a bus conductor who collected fares and issued tickets. As a cost-cutting measure these were reduced so that the driver collected fares from passengers entering the bus. Recently there has been a move to re-introduce conductors.

The tube

The London underground (known as 'the tube') began operating in the 1860s. At the beginning of the twenty-first century, it still provides a crucial service to the capital's commuters (about 2 million people use the tube every day). However, the service is below the standard of that in other European cities. The trains are dirty, very over-crowded especially during rush hours, and there are frequent cancellations. Improving the tube service is a key issue in local politics in London. The government published a 2800-page report arguing that the London underground would operate more efficiently if it depended upon a combination of public and private finance. The trade unions say that this amounts to privatization which will only result in a poorer service as happened with the privatization of the inter-city train services.

Black cabs

Black cab taxis are another symbol of London. Today, many are not black but covered in advertising. They are plentiful in central city areas and are hired by waving at the driver from the street. Mini-cabs are private taxi companies and they cannot be hired on the street – they have to be booked by telephoning the mini-cab office. Whereas the black cab driver will 'have done the knowledge' (a rigorous and detailed test to prove his or her knowledge of London streets), the mini-cab driver will not; and mini-cab companies are subject to minimal regulations. As taxis are quite expensive, they are not used regularly by most people.

A London taxi cab

The Channel tunnel

The Channel tunnel is used by Eurostar to provide a high-speed passenger service between London, Paris and Brussels and by Eurotunnel to provide a shuttle service (Le Shuttle) for cars, motorbikes and buses between Folkestone in England and Calais in France. In the early years after its opening in 1994, it did not compete very successfully with the ferry services which offered a good alternative route across the Channel. The tunnel was expensive and some people felt uneasy about travelling under the sea. However, public perceptions do seem to have changed and business is now thriving. The journey from Waterloo station in central London to Paris takes less than three hours.

Air travel

It is mainly business people who travel by air within England and the UK. International travel is another matter. Heathrow is well-known as the busiest airport in the world for international travellers – it dealt with 64.6 million passengers (excluding those in transit) in the year 2000. To maintain its pre-eminence, it is adding a fifth terminal which it hopes to open in 2006. This is good for Heathrow and for business but not so good for the people who live under the flight-path of the planes. There was enormous popular resentment at the news of the construction of the fifth terminal, and any further extensions to airports around London will face strong local opposition. Many other major English cities also have their own airport. Recently budget airlines, such as easyJet, have begun to offer cheap internal flights. It will be interesting to see how well they can compete with the train services.

Cars

The driving test

As in any country, all drivers have to pass a test and obtain a licence. Those learning to drive obtain a provisional licence which permits them to drive a car around the city streets (not on the motorway) when accompanied by a qualified driver.

The minimum age for car drivers is 17; for drivers of buses, heavy goods vehicles and large motorcycles it is 21.

To obtain your licence you have to take a theory test (questions about the rules of the road, known as 'the Highway Code') and a practical driving test. Many people find the test difficult and have to retake it a number of times. The average pass rate is 46 per cent.

As a result of frequent government campaigns to encourage drivers to reduce speed and improve road safety, travelling by road is getting safer. Between 1981 and 2002 road deaths dropped by 39 per cent and serious casualties fell by 49 per cent, while road traffic rose by 59 per cent. Compared with other EU countries, roads in England are very safe.

The population in England is more densely concentrated in urban areas than in any other country in Europe. Travelling across cities, especially in the rush hours, is best avoided. Everybody complains that there is too much traffic. The fact that most commercial goods are transported by road in England means that the roads are always busy. Some cities are seriously considering the idea of charging drivers to enter city and town centres. Ken Livingstone, the Mayor of London, is proposing to charge £5 to bring cars into the centre of the capital. About 1 million people work in central London and 14 per cent commute by car. At peak times it is thought fifty thousand vehicles an hour enter the city centre. It remains to be seen if such proposals can withstand the inevitable backlash from business and motorists.

Cycling

The government's National Cycling Strategy is intended to increase the number of cyclists and the areas where cyclists can ride their bikes. A national cycling network is being built and is due for completion in 2005. A third of this will be completely free from cars and the rest will be on roads where there will be cycle lanes or measures to favour cyclists.

GLOSSARY

arts examples are literature, theatre, drama

backlash strong reaction to new idea or proposal

budget airlines airline company which specializes in offering very cheap fares

building society type of financial organization which specializes in lending money for house purchase

civil servants people who work for the civil service which is the state organization responsible for putting government plans into effect

commuter a person travelling regularly to and from work

consultant doctor who specializes in treating certain ailments

core subjects the most important subjects

drop-out rate the proportion of students who leave before completing their studies

elite the most powerful and wealthy group in society

first-time buyer someone who is buying their first house

GP General Practitioner: a doctor who provides general medical treatment to people in a particular area. He or she does not work in a hospital

grammar schools secondary schools which select pupils on the basis of their academic ability

'hits' each time someone contacts a website they 'hit' the site, for example, NHS Direct receives 5 million 'hits' a month

mixed ability schooling schools which teach children of different academic abilities

Open University students study part-time for degrees mainly via TV, radio and the Internet

opt out choose not to be involved in something

outpatient person who receives treatment at a hospital but does not stay overnight

residential (nursing) home place where elderly people can live while they are being cared for

rush hours the busiest part of the day when people are starting or finishing work

sixth form college college providing education for 16–18-year-olds

syllabus the subjects studied in a particular course

tutorials small group or individual classes with a tutor

vocational the skills needed for a particular job

Taking it further

Suggested reading

Abercrombie, N and Warde, A, *Contemporary British Society*,
   Polity Press, 2000
HMSO, *Aspects of Britain*   A series of short booklets published
   by the government

Websites

http://www.britishcouncil.org.uk   The British Council provides
   information about studying in England
http://www.shelter.org.uk   Shelter – the National Campaign for
   the Homeless
http://www.nhsdirect.nhs.uk   National Health Service online
   advice
http://www.sustrans.co.uk   Sustrans – sustainable transport – is
   a charity that works on practical projects to encourage people
   to walk, cycle and use public transport in order to reduce motor
   traffic and its adverse effects
http://www.travelengland.org.uk   Travel England – the official
   online guide to England – includes links to other useful
   websites
http://www.ltmuseum.co.uk   The London Transport Museum
http://www.infotransport.co.uk   Travel information about
   trains, buses and planes in the UK
http://www.visitbritain.com   Tourist information for England
   and the rest of Britain
http://www.tourist-boards.com/england.htm   Links to English
   regional tourist boards

10 | THE ENGLISH AT WORK AND PLAY

Changing patterns of work

Economists divide the workforce of a country into those employed in the primary sector of the economy (activity which takes natural resources from the earth or the sea, such as mining, farming and fishing), the secondary sector (manufacturing, for example, car production, shipbuilding, construction) and the tertiary sector (services). Today, most people (about three-quarters) in England work in the service sector of the economy. Examples of service workers are lawyers, insurance and bank workers, hotel workers, shop assistants, hairdressers, call centre workers and nurses. One of the most important changes that has taken place, especially since the 1950s, has been the steady decline in the importance of manufacturing industries. Between 1955 and 2000, the proportion of the total workforce employed in manufacturing fell from 42 to 15 per cent.

The decline of manufacturing

Economic recessions at the start of the 1980s and again in the early 1990s led to a steep reduction in manufacturing capacity. Unlike previous governments, the Conservative government of Mrs Thatcher did not try to prevent troubled industries from declining. In areas where a whole town depended heavily upon one source of work, for example, coal mining areas in the Midlands and the North, the resulting high unemployment meant disaster for the community. There was great economic hardship for those affected by the transformation of the economy (as seen in films set in these times, such as *The Full Monty* and *Billy Elliot*).

Another reason for the decline in manufacturing has been increased overseas competition. Companies in England have been unable to compete with goods produced by less-developed countries, particularly goods from the Far East, where labour is cheaper. Globalization had a negative impact upon certain industries, with production being moved to other countries by multinational organizations in pursuit of lower production costs. In 2002, the Dyson organization, a well-known and successful company based in the west of England, moved production of its household vacuum cleaners to Malaysia with the loss of eight hundred jobs. The move enabled the company to cut production costs by 30 per cent – hourly labour costs in England were £4.10 compared to £1.50 in Malaysia.

The growth of the service sector

Growth in the service sector has been so great in recent years that there are now more people working in Indian restaurants than in shipbuilding, steel manufacturing and in coal mining combined and there are currently three times as many public relations consultants as coal miners. England is now primarily a service-based economy.

Small businesses

Small businesses (companies employing fewer than four people) play an important role in the economy. The majority of organizations fall into this category and they account for about one-fifth of business employment.

The public sector

Another marked change has been the fall in the numbers employed in the public (ie government) sector. This was again in large part due to the privatization programmes of the Conservative government (1979–1997). About one hundred public sector businesses were put into private hands, for example, the telephone, gas, electricity, coal, steel, water and rail services.

A second factor affecting the public sector was 'contracting out'. This is business jargon which means that an organization no longer carries out certain tasks but buys in services from another company. For example, instead of employing people to clean rubbish from the streets, the local government might hire a private firm of cleaners to do the work. Typical 'contracted out' jobs are in catering, cleaning and security.

A third factor that has helped to make the public sector smaller has been the fall in the number of the armed forces; government spending on defence has been reduced significantly since the fall of communism in Central and Eastern Europe.

Information technology

IT is having a profound effect upon employment. For example, in retail banking, large numbers of high street bank branches have closed and been replaced by telephone and Internet banking services. According to one estimate, it is one hundred times cheaper to make a payment through the Internet than with a cheque at a local bank branch. About half of all adults have access to the Internet and the government is encouraging its development. It aims to make the UK a leading e-commerce nation and ensure universal access to the Internet by 2005. Teleworking (people using telephones and computers to work from home) has been increasing too, particularly for journalists, computer programmers and business consultants. Familiarity with e-mail and word processing are now considered basic skills for office workers.

The tourist industry

The government sees tourism as a key growth sector for the future. It provides employment to over 2 million people in bars, pubs, restaurants, hotels, theatres and other places of entertainment. The largest number of visitors to England have traditionally come from the United States, France, Germany, Ireland and Holland. The spread of foot and mouth disease in 2001 had a serious effect upon tourism – as large areas of the country were closed to visitors, many tourists cancelled their holidays. The number of American tourists was further reduced by the events of 11 September 2001.

Cheap package holidays and budget airlines offering very low-cost air travel mean that increasing numbers of people in England look overseas, especially to the Mediterranean sunshine, for their holidays (see page 208), with consequent effects upon the tourist industry at home. However, when English people take a summer holiday in England they often go to seaside destinations such as Blackpool, Bournemouth, and places in Devon and Cornwall. Historic cities like York, Bath, Cambridge, Oxford and Durham are also popular with tourists from all over the world

The seafront at Blackpool

Agriculture

Agriculture provides work for only about 1 to 2 per cent of the total labour force, which is small by comparison with many other European countries. However, the total number of people who depend on farming for their employment and livelihood is in fact much greater if we include all those who work in food preparation and the transportation of food and animals, as well as those employed in food retail, such as butcher's shops and supermarkets.

About 80 per cent of the land in England is used for agriculture, compared with 42 per cent for the European Union as a whole. A wide variety of crops are cultivated: wheat and barley taking up most land. Other significant activities include horticulture and the cultivation of oilseed rape, sugar beet, peas and beans.

The weather may change every day in England but there are few extremes of temperature and this is good for farming. Generally, English farms are very productive. Yields are high and farmers can supply about 60 per cent of the country's food. More than half of farms are predominantly concerned with rearing livestock or are dairy farms. Cattle and sheep are mostly found in hilly or moorland parts of northern and south-western England. Farms which depend largely on arable crops are located mainly in eastern and central-southern England.

Agricultural exports (such as cereals, pork, poultry, dairy products and sugar) go mostly to the European Union (especially France, the Irish Republic, Germany and Spain). However, there is a significant amount of business with the United States and Japan.

Compared to other countries in Europe, English farms are big; in 1995 the average farm was 70 hectares (ie about the size of 140 football pitches) which is almost double the size of farms in the countries with the next biggest farms, Luxembourg and Denmark, and about four times bigger than the size of the average farm in the European Union as a whole. However, in the 1990s an unfortunate combination of factors created a profound crisis in the industry.

The crisis in agriculture

Between 1995 and 2000 farmers' incomes dropped by 90 per cent. A typical family farm that earned £80,000 per year in 1995, was earning just £8000 a year by 2000. In some cases the prices obtained for food produced by the farmers fell below the cost of production. Between June 1998 and June 1999, twenty-two thousand farmers and farm workers lost their jobs. One major reason for the crisis was the strength of the British currency. This made foreign imports cheaper and British exports less competitive. It has made it especially difficult to export to Europe. Furthermore, like most farmers in the European Union, British farmers receive a subsidy under the European Common Agricultural Policy. As this is calculated in Euros, the strength of the British pound further reduced the value of the financial support provided.

Concern about food safety has been another problem. The discovery of bovine spongiform encephalopathy (BSE or 'mad cow disease') led to a worldwide ban on the export of British beef.

Then, in 2001, when farmers were just beginning to recover from the effects of BSE, there was an outbreak of 'foot and mouth' disease. The government's method for controlling the spread of this disease was to kill all the animals that were infected or that might have been infected. On some farms all the animals were killed. Not surprisingly, consumer confidence in British meat suffered badly and many farmers were simply unable to earn a living.

Small farms were especially badly affected by the crisis. Many went bankrupt, further reducing working opportunities in the countryside. The agricultural workforce fell by over 10 per cent in the early 1990s and younger people sought jobs outside farming. The average age of farmers is 57 years old. About one-quarter of all farms are owned by someone over 65 and only 6 per cent by someone under 35.

Organic farming

A notable development resulting from the food scares has been the increase in demand for organic food (food grown without the aid of pesticides or intensive farming methods) and the growth of organic farms. Only about 3 per cent of land is organic at the moment but the government is providing money to assist farmers who are willing to change.

Some farmers have tried to diversify into other areas to bring in extra income, often into some form of rural tourism, such as providing bed and breakfast accommodation to holiday-makers. Yet, many people have had to move away from the countryside and seek employment in the cities. This has led to a significant decline in services in the countryside, for example, a reduction in shops, post offices, pubs, schools, banks and doctors.

Urban attitudes to the crisis

These are somewhat mixed. On the one hand, most people feel sympathetic about the real distress being suffered by farmers. An industry and a whole way of life are under threat. The countryside and the concept of village life is associated by many with symbolic and romantic notions of 'old' England. One of the most popular programmes on the radio is a soap opera about life in the countryside. This is *The Archers* which has been broadcast regularly on BBC radio since the early 1950s. The Countryside Alliance, an organization which campaigns on behalf of rural interests, is demanding more government help to preserve the rural economy.

On the other hand, it can be argued that agriculture is a comparatively small sector of the national economy and other larger industries, such as the coal or iron and steel industries were allowed to decline when they were no longer viable in the 1980s. Moreover, farming has been benefiting from European Union subsidies for a long time. The European Union's Common Agricultural Policy is a controversial issue in England. Farmers benefit from the subsidies, but according to UK government calculations, families pay £16 a week extra in grocery prices and taxes as a result. The original aim when the policy started was to bring stability to European Union farm prices and a decent income to farmers. European farmers make more food than they can sell and the surplus is bought by the European Union to sustain prices. All in all, the future for the farming industry in England looks bleak.

Fishing

The English fishing industry provides about half of the country's needs and is an important source of employment in a number of sea ports, mainly in the south-west and on the east coast. However, there have been problems caused by arguments about ships from other countries fishing illegally in English waters. English fishermen complain that ships from other countries are breaking the European Union laws about where to fish and how much fish can be caught.

Working practices

Today, few employees can expect guaranteed job security, as employers now favour 'workplace flexibility'. In practice, this means that, instead of employing staff on permanent contracts, as they did in the past, employers now make greater use of temporary workers, fixed-term and part-time contracts. Businesses are financially more efficient but workers often feel less secure and more worried about unemployment or redundancy. And this can affect the middle as well as the working classes. In the past, jobs such as a university lecturer or a bank manager would have been considered a job for life, but this is not the case any more.

Working hours

Most full-time employees work a basic forty-hour, five-day week. For part-time workers the average is sixteen hours per week. In comparison with other European countries, men and women full-time employees in England spend more time at work. Agriculture, construction, transport and communications have the longest working day; the shortest is in public administration, education and health. About 20 per cent of people now work on 'flexitime', ie employees can vary the start and finish times, provided an agreed amount of hours are spent at work each day or each week.

Paid holidays

The average paid holiday entitlement for full-time employees is about five weeks. Temporary and part-time workers may have fewer holidays. Bank holidays are supposed to be days when the City and financial institutions, such as the banks, closed. If banks closed, then the assumption was that all other businesses would close too and consequently workers would have a holiday. In the past, commercial life came to a standstill on bank holidays. Not any longer. According to a recent survey (Labour Force Survey 2000), 31.5 per cent of all employees work at least one bank holiday during the year. Rates of pay are higher for working on public holidays (see Chapter Six). Nowadays, shops and restaurants usually open as normal. England never really closes. Retailing is particularly important in this respect because if the shops open late seven days a week, then there are consequences for transport and delivery services, catering, communications and entertainment. But work is not simply about earning money or advancing your career – research suggests that a third of people's good friendships are made at work and half of all English people meet their partners there.

Sick leave

According to a government study, social workers take more days off work because of illness than any other occupation. They are followed by the men and women examiners who carry out driving tests. Most healthy or conscientious are doctors who take only 2.9 days off work per year.

Days off work per year	
Social services	15
Driving examiners	14.3
Police	11.5
Average	7.8
Banking	7
Manufacturing	6.9
Retailing	5.8
Teachers	5
Doctors	2.9
(source: *Metro*, 25 June 2001)	

Earnings and take-home pay

Earnings vary considerably. Agriculture, fishing, and the hotel and restaurant sector have traditionally been low paid. At the other end of the pay scale, workers in finance and business earn relatively high rates of pay. People in London do earn more than northerners who perform similar types of work, but the cost of living in the capital is greater: average income in London is over £24,000 per year for men and about £15,000 for women; but in the north-east the figures are £16,000 for men and about £9000 for women (source: Inland Revenue 1997–8). Indeed, some analysts think that London is one of the most expensive cities in the world. A survey by the bank UBS Warburg examined costs and standards of living in fifty-eight cities around the world. London was the tenth most expensive city based on the cost of a range of goods but ranked twenty-third in the standard of living league table, behind other major European and US cities.

In 2002 the national minimum wage was £3.50 per hour for 18–21 year olds and £4.10 for anyone over 22. Almost all workers are covered by this legislation; there are no exceptions for casual workers, temporary, part-time or overseas workers. About 1.5 million people, two-thirds of whom were women, became entitled to higher wages when the minimum wage was introduced on 1 April 1999. This change had most impact on people in hotels and catering, shops, cleaning, care work, clothing manufacture and private security work.

Earnings and take-home pay are not the same thing. Although a person might earn, for example, £1600 a month, they will actually receive significantly less than that from their employer. There will be deductions for income tax, national insurance and perhaps the company pension scheme.

Income taxes

These are frequently considered high by the general public but in fact they are not when compared to most other European countries. An individual can earn a certain amount (£4535), called 'personal allowance', before they pay any tax. There are also certain other allowances, for example, for being over 65 years of age and for having children. The rate of taxation is 'progressive', ie the more money you earn, the more you pay. Most people (about two-thirds) pay tax at the basic rate.

Bands of taxable income (2001–2002)	
Starting rate of 10%	£ 0–1880
Basic rate of 22%	£1880–29,400
Higher rate of 40%	over £29,400
[Note: These can be varied by the annual budget.]	

There have been significant changes in tax over time. Mostly, there have been reductions in income tax and an increase in indirect taxes (eg sales tax) which have generally benefited the wealthier. At the height of their fame in the 1960s, the Beatles were paying the higher rate of tax which was then 98 per cent! They complained by writing a song ('Taxman') about it. The basic rate in the 1960s was 40 per cent; it fell to 30 per cent in the 1980s and then later in the 1990s to 23 per cent. This partly helps to explain why statistics show that the rich have been getting richer because they have a higher disposable income.

For employed people, who are the majority of the workforce, tax is deducted from their wages or salary by their employer and forwarded to the tax authorities (the Inland Revenue). This is known as PAYE – the Pay As You Earn scheme. However, if you are self-employed, you pay 'lump sums' twice a year.

National insurance

Employees pay about 10 per cent of their earnings to the government in national insurance. This is matched by a similar amount from the employer. National insurance contributions are compulsory and cover the cost of benefits such as retirement pension and the Jobseeker's allowance.

The black economy

If you want to have your house decorated or your car fixed, you may need a builder or a car mechanic to do the work. The builder or decorator should under most circumstances pay tax and VAT (valued added tax, 17.5 per cent) on money charged for the work. When tax is not paid we are in the world of the black economy. Accurate figures about the size of the black economy are impossible to obtain but the Inland Revenue estimates that millions of pounds owed to the government are lost every year.

Unemployment

During most of the 1990s unemployment was low (about 5 per cent of the workforce) compared with other countries in Europe. However, this general figure hides significant variations across the country: from 4.6 per cent in the south-east to 11.9 per cent in Merseyside in the north-west in 2001. For young people under 25, unemployment is double the national rate.

For the first six months of unemployment, people normally receive a Jobseeker's allowance ('the dole') – about £54 a week in 2002. After that, they may receive some money but the amount is income-related, ie it depends on how much money they have saved and/or if they have other sources of income. In other words, the more money a person has in the bank, the less money they will receive from the government.

Women in the workplace

Today the majority of women (about 75 per cent) in England who are of working age (16–65 years) are in employment.

There have been two long-term trends in women's patterns of employment over the last one hundred years:

- **The increase in the number of working women**: at the beginning of the twentieth century, women were about one-third of the workforce but by the end of the 1990s this figure had risen to nearly half. Mostly, this increase has been among married women. Less than one-tenth of married women were working in the early twentieth century, compared with three-quarters by 2001.

- **The growth in part-time work**: the overwhelming majority of part-time workers are female. Many choose part-time work in order to fit in with their family obligations. Although social attitudes have changed during the last one hundred years, research suggests that women still take most of the responsibility for housework and childcare. Getting the kids off to school in the morning and then being at home for them returning in the late afternoon limits the hours available for employment. There are still few workplaces today with childcare facilities which would allow working mothers to take full-time jobs.

Inequality in pay and conditions

Legislation was created over thirty years ago to prevent discrimination because of gender. Of course, the law applies to men and women equally, but in practice it mostly concerns discrimination against women. Although these legal measures had some influence at first, significant inequalities still persist. For example, on average, women earn about 20–25 per cent less than men. The difference is explained by men taking jobs with higher rates of pay and longer hours of work.

**Average gross weekly earnings (full-time)
of men and women**

Men	£414
Women	£301.30

(source: Government Statistical service, *The UK in Figures / Regional Statistics*, April 1997)

The sexual division of labour: breaking through 'the glass ceiling'

In England, women can now be found doing every kind of job, yet they predominate in certain areas – this is what is called 'the sexual division of labour'. The ratio of females to males in clerical and secretarial jobs is 4:1, and women are strongly represented in teaching, nursing and other service sector jobs. There are twice as many men as women working as managers and senior staff.

This sexual division of labour is one reason for the difference in earnings. The kind of jobs women do tend to be less well paid. However, even where men and women are working in the same job, women tend not to be promoted; they come up against the so-called 'glass ceiling', the invisible barrier of prejudice that prevents women's progress up the organizational hierarchy.

However, this situation may be changing. The Labour government is trying to encourage employers to accept more flexible working practices to allow women to take career breaks or work part-time while bringing up children. In addition, there is evidence that women are becoming more outspoken against unfair treatment. Since 1995, the number of equal pay cases registered with tribunals (courts which deal with cases of alleged discrimination) has more than doubled.

Year	Total number of cases
1995	694
1998	1530

(source: The Equal Opportunities Commission)

The position of women improved enormously during the twentieth century, particularly during the period 1970–1980 as a result of the influence of the Women's Movement. Social attitudes have altered, sexism has become much less acceptable and women have become more assertive. However, they still earn less than men, have poorer career opportunities and have less job security.

Trade unions

Trade unions represent their members in discussions with employers about pay and conditions of work as well as providing legal advice on work-related matters and educational facilities. There is a long tradition of trade union membership and activity in England stretching back well into the nineteenth century.

In 2002, just under 30 per cent of the workforce were members of a trade union; only a slightly higher proportion of men than women are members. Trade union members are more likely to be found among older employees and those in the public sector. Union membership was much higher in the past but has been declining steadily over the last twenty years. A number of reasons account for this. There has been a sharp drop in the number of employees in industries where membership had been traditionally high, such as manufacturing and coal mining. There has also been a fall in full-time employment and an increase in part-time, casual and temporary work. These types of workers are less likely to join unions. The Conservative government (1979–1997), which was generally hostile to unions, introduced legislation making it harder for them to function. For example, the 'closed shop' agreement between employer and trade union was no longer possible; such agreements had meant that only union members could be hired by the company. In addition, formal ballots of workers before a strike were made obligatory.

The most important organization in the trade union movement is the TUC (Trades Union Congress) which was set up in 1868 and represents most of the biggest unions; seventy-four unions are associated with the TUC and these amount to nearly 7 million people. UNISON is the largest union and represents local government and National Health Service workers.

Historically, many unions have been closely allied with the Labour Party. Indeed, the Labour Party still receives much of its funding from the unions. However, along with a decline in membership, trade unions have experienced a decline in political influence. This was high in the 1960s and 1970s when union leaders were regularly consulted by government ministers. Indeed, the miners' strike of 1974 is credited with bringing down the Conservative administration and causing a general election. Times have changed, and union leaders are no longer such powerful figures on the political stage.

Strikes

During the period from the 1950s to the 1980s strikes became so common that the country gained an international reputation for being strike-prone. The miners' strike of 1984 was a particularly bitter dispute, occasionally involving violent confrontations between strikers and police. In the end, the miners lost their battle with the government and this signalled a significant change in labour relations. It felt like a defeat for the trade union movement as a whole. Since that time, there has been a steep decline in strike activity and the climate of management-worker relations has changed. Fewer days were lost from strikes in the first part of the 1990s than in any other decade since 1900, and the figure for 1997 was the smallest since records began in 1891.

Children and work

Officially, children must stay at school until they are 16 years old and then are allowed to start working full-time. Children who are 13 or 14 can work for two hours a day on weekdays and five hours on Saturdays. Fifteen-year-olds are allowed to work eight hours on a Saturday. However, most children do not go to work. For those who do, the work might consist of, for example, working in a shop on a Saturday. Doing an early morning paper round before school starts is another way of earning some extra pocket money.

Leisure time

In common with other parts of Europe, patterns of leisure seem to be changing so that free-time is more frequently spent inside the home. The English are spending less time on visits to the pub or the cinema and more indoors, probably watching TV or involved in DIY.

Typical English pub

Home-based activities

■ The most popular home-based activity is watching television (about twenty-five hours per week for each person). The BBC, ITV1 and Channel Four are available to everybody with a TV set, and many viewers now receive Channel 5, which was launched in 1997. Cable and satellite TV have added to the number of stations available – about three out of ten homes have access to satellite television. Soap operas, like *Coronation Street* on ITV1 and *Eastenders* on BBC1 regularly attract millions of viewers when they are broadcast about three times a week. *Coronation Street* must be one of the longest running TV programmes in the world – it began in 1960! In a poll carried out by the British Film Institute in 2000, *Fawlty Towers* (comedy) with John Cleese was voted the all-time favourite television programme.

- The second most popular activity is visiting and entertaining friends or relations.
- DIY or Do-It-Yourself may not be everyone's idea of fun, but it has become an increasingly popular hobby, as testified by the many TV 'make-over' programmes which show viewers how to transform their house or garden.
- Listening to music and buying CDs and tapes is as popular as ever. In 2001, 'Hear'say' became the first band to have number one best-sellers in both the singles and the album charts simultaneously with their debut releases. They were successful mainly because they were formed out of a TV talent show competition.
- Many people still read a daily newspaper. The most popular by far is *The Sun*.
- A famous English writer, GK Chesterton, said that England was a country where the word 'God' was spelt backwards, ie 'Dog'. England is a nation of pet lovers. About half of all households own a pet; dogs and cats are the most popular. In recent years the cat population has grown larger than the dog population. This may reflect changes in lifestyle – there is less time to give dogs the attention they need. Most people, whether living on their own, or in a couple, are out at work all day.

Activities outside the home

- Going to the pub is the most popular leisure activity outside the home. Pubs open at about 11.00 a.m. but most people would only visit their 'local' for a drink in the evening. Many now offer good food too and Sunday lunch is always popular.
- 'Retail therapy' – a newspaper survey found that 20 per cent of women are compulsive shoppers. Increasing numbers of young men also enjoy shopping.
- For holidays, Majorca is the most popular destination, while France is the most popular for short breaks (two or three days). The area preferred by people holidaying in Britain is the West Country. The proportion of people taking two or more holidays increased from 15 to 25 per cent between 1971 and 1998.

■ Sport and physical recreation have always been popular. Local government is the main provider of cheap and basic sport leisure facilities, such as tennis courts, parks, athletics grounds, golf courses and swimming pools. There are many private sports clubs and gyms providing sporting facilities but these can often be very expensive.

Popular sports, games and physical activities
% participation by those aged 16 and over

Men		Women	
Walking	49	Walking	41
Snooker/pool/billiards	19	Keep fit/yoga	17
Cycling	15	Swimming	16
Swimming	13	Cycling	8
Soccer	10	Snooker/pool/billiards	4

■ Every year thousands take part in the London Marathon (thirty-two thousand competitors in 2002) and the Great North Run in Newcastle upon Tyne. The runners include a number of serious athletes competing to win but for most people it is just healthy (and exhausting) fun including some people dressed in silly costumes. Many ask friends to sponsor them and raise money for charity.

■ Cricket is played regularly during the summer months. There is a professional league and Test (international) matches are played every summer. It is still played regularly in schools and colleges and by local amateur teams.

■ Field sports take place in the countryside. These include shooting birds and hunting wild animals like foxes. Organizations like the Countryside Alliance view these as legitimate pastimes, but other people, including animal rights campaigners, think they are cruel and should be banned. It is a controversial topic and it seems quite possible that in the near future some field sports will either be made illegal or severely restricted.

■ The impression you might get from the media is that the whole country is football crazy. This may appear to be the case at certain times, eg during the World Cup competition, when it is an inescapable topic of conversation. However, at other times it is a minority interest. Manchester United has the largest number of people attending their matches. Their average home gate is fifty-five thousand. It is the favourite team among young people aged 7–16 except in the north-east of the country and London. Football has grown in popularity with women – 14 per cent of fans watching football in the Premier League are female. Only 0.9 per cent of football season ticket holders are black or Asian.

- Rugby football takes its name from Rugby school where it was first played. There are two variations of the game, with slightly different rules. Rugby Union involves fifteen players in each team and is most popular in the south-west. Rugby League which involves only thirteen players in each team is more popular in the north and has more working-class associations.

- The origins of modern tennis date back to England in the 1870s and the first championship competitions were played in Wimbledon in 1877. An estimated 5 million people play tennis. Tennis courts are available to rent in many public parks and for those willing to spend more money there are plenty of private tennis clubs.

- About two-thirds of adults gamble at least once a year. Most of these are people who buy National Lottery tickets and dream of becoming a millionaire. Betting on horse races, especially the Derby and the Grand National which take place once a year, is also popular.

GLOSSARY

call centre companies which deal with customer requests on the telephone. Particularly popular with banking, insurance and retailing services

the City financial district in the centre of London

disposable income amount of salary left after deducting taxes, housing costs and other basic needs

DIY abbreviation for Do-It-Yourself. Decorating your home yourself rather than employing someone else to do it

fixed-term contract contract of employment lasting a specified time, such as one year

funding financial support, money

home gate the number of people attending a football match when the team is playing at its own ground

horticulture study and practice of growing plants and cultivating gardens

indirect tax tax on goods and services

Inland Revenue government organization which deals with tax

livestock animals on a farm

local expression sometimes used to refer to a nearby and frequently visited pub

moorland high open land with rough grass and heather

nationalized owned by the state

pocket money money which parents give to their children each week or month and which the children can spend on themselves

soap opera radio or television programme about the daily lives of a group of people

yield the amount of food produced

Taking it further

Suggested reading

Scase, R, *Britain in 2010*, Capstone Publishing, 2000
    A fascinating guide to future developments and trends
Office of National Statistics, *Britain 2000: The Official Handbook of the United Kingdom*, The Stationery Office, Norwich   This is updated every year and, although produced by the government, it provides a generally well-balanced and comprehensive overview
Halsey, A H and Webb, J, *Twentieth-century British Social Trends*, Palgrave Macmillan, 2000

Websites

http://www.countryside-alliance.org   Organization promoting the countryside
http://www.travelengland.org.uk   The English Tourist Board website
http://www.ecb.co.uk   The English and Welsh cricket board
http://www.timeout.com   Information about events in London

11 | THE PEOPLE AND THEIR ENVIRONMENT

Population

The total population of England today is about 50 million, an increase of nearly two-thirds compared with its population of just over 30 million in 1901, and it is expected to go on growing for at least the next thirty years. Though there were baby booms after both the First and Second World Wars, the birth rate has generally gone down throughout this period. The average number of children a woman has is now only 1.73, less than the number needed to keep the population constant, and this means that the proportion of young people in the population is falling. However, the number of people living in England is going up, and will continue to go up, and there are three main reasons why this is so.

- First of all, better standards of living and better healthcare mean that far fewer babies die young. Even in the last twenty years, there has been a change from one in a hundred babies dying before their first birthday, to less than six in every thousand today.
- Secondly, people are living much longer. A baby boy born today can expect to live until he is 75, and a baby girl until she is 80 (compared with 49 and 53 a hundred years ago), and life expectancy for both men and women is still rising, though it is going up faster for men at the moment. This means that the proportion of the population who are over the normal retirement age is steadily increasing. In 1901, one person in twenty was over 65; today it is one in six. That trend is expected to continue, and in fifteen years' time, there will probably be more people over 65 than under 16.
- Thirdly, more people come into the country as immigrants than leave it to live elsewhere; in fact about two-thirds of the current

increase in the size of the population is caused by immigration, which is discussed in more detail in the next section.

Who are the English?

What does it mean to be English in the twenty-first century? Visitors to London often comment on how ethnically mixed it seems. When you walk the streets or travel on the underground, you cannot help noticing how many people there are who come – or whose ancestors came – from Africa or the Caribbean, or from south Asia. Many other cities also seem quite mixed. Overall, though, about 93 per cent of the population is white, though this does not necessarily mean that their families have always lived in England. There has always been a good deal of migration into England from Scotland, Wales and Ireland, and more recently from many other parts of Europe as well.

The ethnic mix	
	%
White	93
Black (Caribbean, African etc)	2
South Asian (Indian, Bangladeshi and Pakistani)	3.5
Chinese	0.3
Other non-white groups	1.2
(Source: *UK 2002 Yearbook*)	

The idea of 'Englishness' is now a very complex one; while some people feel that the English are those of white Anglo-Saxon origin, others include everyone born in England, whatever their racial origin. This is further complicated by the fact that many children of immigrants consider themselves to be British rather than English.

Where people live

England is the second most densely populated country in Europe after the Netherlands. It has about three hundred and eighty people per square kilometre, compared with one hundred and forty-one in Wales and only sixty-five in Scotland. But this average figure hides some big regional differences. About 15.5 million people, nearly a third of the total population, live in London and the rest of the south-east. More prosperous areas such as the Midlands and the south-east attract people away from older industrial areas in the northern parts of England, as well as from Wales and Scotland. The tendency for people to move away from the rural areas and into towns and cities, which began during the industrial revolution more than two hundred years ago, is still continuing. However, there is also a tendency for people to move out of the inner city areas and into the suburbs. This trend has slowed a little in recent years, with a number of schemes to regenerate inner cities. A good example of this is the area in the eastern part of London where the docks used to be. Old warehouses along the banks of the River Thames have been converted into flats and offices, and areas that were derelict and decaying are now lively and thriving again.

Age differences

When we look at the distribution of the population by age, we notice some interesting regional differences. The population of London is, in fact, slowly going down in all age-groups except for young people aged 15–24 who are growing in number, which means that the total number of people living in London is actually going up. In the south-west, on the other hand, all age-groups are increasing their numbers – except for the 15–24s, who are declining. These two figures probably reflect the difference in the availability of jobs for young people in the two areas. All along the south coast of England, the proportion of old people is much higher than elsewhere. This is because the mild climates of the southern seaside towns make them attractive places for older people to move to when they retire.

The Census

Where do we get all this information about the population? Every ten years since 1801, a census is conducted; every household in the country is asked to make a list of the full names of all the people living at that address, and each person has to give other details such as their ages and professions. The questions asked change a little each time. In 1991, people were asked for the first time to say what ethnic group they belonged to, and in the 2001 census a question about religion was included for the first time since 1851. Statistics based on the census are published by the government as soon as they have been analyzed, a year or so after the census date. But the information given by individuals is kept secret for a hundred years. The Public Record Office recently put the detailed results of the 1901 census on its website, but it was so popular with people who were interested in tracing their ancestors that the site had to be closed down for a while. (Tracing family history is one of the most popular Internet activities in England.)

Immigration

For hundreds of years, people have come from other countries to settle in England. In general, England has been sympathetic to people who were being persecuted in their own countries, from French Protestants (known as the Huguenots) in the late seventeenth century to Jewish refugees who came from eastern Europe in the late nineteenth century and from Germany in the 1930s. In the early 1970s, people of Asian origin were expelled from Uganda, and many of those with British passports fled to the UK.

Many people have also come to live in England for economic reasons. During the 1950s and early 1960s, there was a serious labour shortage in England, especially in the health service, public transport and catering, as well as in some industries such as textiles. The government therefore encouraged people to immigrate from the Caribbean and the Indian sub-continent (India, Pakistan and Bangladesh) to fill these job vacancies. They tended to live in the poorer areas of London and other big cities where the labour shortages were, and where housing was cheapest. It was also natural for later arrivals to move to areas where there were already communities from their home country.

The English have always had rather mixed attitudes towards foreigners, and some found it difficult to accept such large numbers of immigrants, especially as they were in many ways much more distinctively different from earlier immigrant groups. Not only were they racially different, but some also spoke their own languages, and kept the religion and culture of their original country. Many found themselves discriminated against. They had the worst housing and the lowest-paid jobs, and they were often abused by whites. Some right-wing politicians warned that there would be violent conflict between different racial groups if immigration continued, and some even campaigned for immigrants to be returned to their countries of origin.

Legislation

The government reacted by introducing two different types of legislation. The Immigration Act 1971 made it more difficult for people to come to the UK as immigrants, and these restrictions were further strengthened by the Immigration and Asylum Act 1999. Many people felt that this legislation was intended to cut down the number of immigrants from ethnic minorities, although this was not stated.

The Race Relations Act 1976 (amended in 2000) made it illegal to discriminate against anyone on the grounds of their race, and covers many areas of life, including employment and education. The original Act also set up the Commission for Racial Equality (CRE) as an independent organization to enforce the legislation against racial discrimination and to promote racial equality. In practice it is not easy to stop discrimination simply by passing a law. But over the years the majority of the white population has come to see that discrimination is unacceptable, though race riots in Oldham, Bradford and Burnley in the north of England in the summer of 2001 show that there are still many problems.

In recent years, refugees have come to England to escape war or persecution in the Balkan states, Afghanistan, Iraq and Iran, as well as a number of other countries. They are initially referred to as 'asylum seekers', reflecting uncertainty about the real reasons for their applications for refugee status. Many are considered to be 'economic migrants' and less than a quarter of those who apply are given refugee status or are allowed to stay in the UK for some other reason.

A recent report for the British government says that although immigration increased considerably in the 1990s and is now the main factor affecting population change, the UK has a lower proportion of immigrants than most countries in the EU – in 1998 it was only 3.8 per cent of the total population of the UK. The report also found that foreign workers are generally more highly skilled than the average in the UK, and so benefit the UK economy.

The family

The stereotypical English family consists of a mother, a father (married, of course) and two children. This is the so-called 'nuclear' family. Although both politicians and the media talk about changing ideas about 'the family' in England today, about three-quarters of people living in private households are still in 'couple families'. On the surface this looks as if the traditional family has survived as strongly as ever, but a closer look shows us that there have been some quite dramatic changes. First of all, it has become much more common for couples to live together without marrying. Many couples never marry, while others live together (or cohabit) for some time before eventually marrying. It is not unusual for those who do marry to wait until *after* at least the first child has been born. And secondly, the children may include the children of one or both parents from a previous relationship, as in this example:

> *Susie lives with her dad, Tom, and his second wife Maggie – and also with her two step-sisters Megan and Chloë (Maggie's daughters from her first marriage) as well as her little half-brother Josh who is Tom and Maggie's son. Susie's mum lives with her new partner, Mike, and their daughter Gemma who is Susie's half-sister.*

The majority of people still get married, though the proportion has steadily decreased, and a recently-published survey suggests that married people will soon be a minority in England. Twenty years ago, around 74 per cent of women under 50 were married; now only about 50 per cent are. The proportions for men are slightly higher, but the trend is similar, showing that marriage is very much in decline.

Legal marital status of women aged 18–49		
	1979	**2000**
	%	%
Married	74	51
Single	18	35
Divorced	4	9
Separated	3	5

Note: The number of widows in this age-group is insignificant

(Source: *Living in Britain 2000, The Office of National Statistics*)

As you can see from the table above, the change in the proportion of married women cannot be explained by the increased rate of divorce and separation. It is caused by the fact that women are either marrying much later or not at all. Thirty years ago, the average age of a woman marrying for the first time was 22 (24 for a man), but by 1999 this had risen to 27 (29 for a man).

The divorce rate has also steadily increased since the 1960s, though in the last few years the number has declined. Since there are fewer marriages overall, fewer are likely to end in divorce.

During the same period, the proportions of people who live together without being married, or who live in one-parent families, or who live alone, have all increased. Most single-parent families are headed by women: 23 per cent of all families have lone mothers, while lone-father families make up only 3 per cent of the total. And a staggering 32 per cent of all households now consist of only one person, nearly twice as many as thirty years ago.

All of these changes are related to one very significant change in social attitudes in England, and that is the change in attitudes to sex, and the related issues of abortion and birth outside marriage. When people were asked recently whether they thought it was wrong for a man and woman to have sexual relations outside marriage, nearly 60 per cent said it was not wrong at all. It is a small step from that to believing that it is also quite acceptable for people to have children outside marriage; the great majority of children born outside marriage are born to parents who live together.

Roles of the sexes

Many women put off starting a family until they are in their late twenties or early thirties. This gives them time to establish themselves in a career first. Some women stay at home until their youngest child starts school, others go back to work as soon as their maternity leave is over, relying on relatives, childminders or nurseries for childcare. Increasing numbers of larger employers provide workplace crèches so that parents can bring their pre-school children to work with them.

Thirty years ago, the vast majority of mothers were housewives. Now it is unusual for a mother not to work, at least once the children are all of school age. The reasons for this change are complex. Women are more highly educated now, and are less likely to feel satisfied with a purely domestic role. Because they may have worked for quite a long time before having a family, they have become used to being financially independent. Also, many families feel they cannot manage on only one income; the cost of housing is very high, whether rented or owned. Perhaps, too, people expect a much higher standard of living than in the past.

Because so many women work, men are now expected to be much more actively involved in childcare and housework. Nevertheless, primary responsibility still seems to rest with women.

Care of the elderly

Many older people live alone, mostly from choice rather than necessity. People value their independence, and generally prefer to stay in their own homes as long as they can, rather than live with relatives. But families often live nearby and provide support, and both social services and voluntary organizations like Age Concern or Help the Aged provide domestic services like cleaning, or 'meals-on-wheels', as well as day centres where elderly people can enjoy a range of social activities and a cooked meal at lunchtime. Because most women work, it is no longer easy for them to provide full-time care for elderly relatives who are too frail to live alone. In such cases, the elderly person usually moves to a residential home or a nursing home.

Religion

The majority of people in England say they believe in God or a higher power of some kind, yet only a small proportion regularly attend religious services. Since Roman times, the main religion in England has been Christianity, but church attendance has been declining since the Second World War. During the 1990s alone there was a drop of 22 per cent, and now less than 8 per cent of the population attend church on Sunday. A much higher percentage attend services on special occasions such as ceremonies to mark births, marriages and deaths, or to celebrate religious festivals. The churches are always full at Christmas and Easter, for example, and about 40 per cent of marriages involve a religious ceremony.

There is also a long-established but declining Jewish community, and growing numbers of Muslims, Sikhs, Hindus and Buddhists (see page 223).

The Church of England and the State

As we saw in Chapter One, the Reformation of the Church in the time of King Henry VIII created great divisions within the Christian Church. Henry rejected the authority of the Pope and the Roman Catholic Church, and made himself head of the Church of England which gradually became more Protestant in its beliefs. The divisions between Protestants and Catholics continued for a long time, and played a significant part in the Civil War in the time of King Charles I. Even now, the king or queen must be a member of the Church of England, and is not allowed to marry a Roman Catholic.

Ever since Henry VIII, the monarch has always been head or 'Supreme Governor' of the Church of England, which is referred to as the 'established' church. This means the official or state church, and until the middle of the nineteenth century anyone who wanted to go to university or hold public office had to belong to it. In fact it was only as recently as 2001 that a law was finally passed to allow a Catholic priest to become a Member of Parliament. Today religious belief is considered to be a private matter for the individual, and there is complete religious freedom.

Political influence

However, the Church of England still has considerable political influence (the two archbishops and the twenty-four most senior bishops are members of the House of Lords), and the state is still involved in important decisions about the Anglican Church. As we write this book, the Archbishop of Canterbury, who is the senior cleric in the Church of England, has just announced that he intends to retire, and the process of choosing a successor has begun. A committee of senior members of the Church, with a chairperson appointed by the prime minister, will consider all the possible candidates and then present two names to the prime minister who will recommend one of them to the Queen for her approval. So in the end it will be a political decision rather than a religious one.

A 'broad' church?

In terms of numbers, the Church of England is the largest of the Christian churches in England. It sometimes claims to be a 'broad' church, by which it means that it includes a wide range of views and religious practices from 'high church' which is similar to the Catholic Church, to 'low church', where the beliefs and practices are close to those of the more evangelical Christian denominations. The Anglican Church was deeply divided during the 1990s about whether to allow women to become priests. Eventually a compromise solution was worked out, so that women could become priests, but those priests and bishops who were opposed to the idea were able to avoid having anything to do with them.

Catholicism in England

The Roman Catholic Church has the second largest membership of all the churches in England. It was effectively banned from the seventeenth century until 1850, with only a very small number of families still practising Catholicism during that time. Once the ban was lifted, the Church grew rapidly, particularly amongst working-class people and Irish immigrants. But like the Anglican Church, attendance at Sunday services is declining.

Other Christian denominations

The other Christian denominations in England differ from the Anglican and Catholic Churches in having no bishops. They are known as the 'non-conformist' churches, and include the Methodist, Baptist, Pentecostal and United Reformed Churches, as well as some smaller denominations. Though nearly all of these have declining participation, some of the newer, more informal and more evangelistic groups have been growing, particularly amongst the ethnic minority communities in London.

Other faiths in England

The non-Christian religions in England are found mainly amongst the ethnic minorities and were originally brought by immigrants, although nowadays most of their followers are British-born.

The oldest distinctive group of immigrants are the Jews, who started to arrive in England from Spain and Portugal in the seventeenth century and were followed by refugees from Central and Eastern Europe during the nineteenth and twentieth centuries. Their numbers are relatively small, and those who regularly attend synagogue are even fewer. There are two groups of Jews, Orthodox and Progressive, representing more conservative or more liberal interpretations of Judaism.

Regent's Park Mosque

The largest non-Christian religion in England today is Islam. There are around 1.5 million Muslims, and their numbers have been growing rapidly. As with most other religions, there are different groups within Islam. Some see a need to modernize and achieve a compromise between religious and secular values, while those in the more fundamentalist groups reject the values of the West entirely. These are a minority at the moment, but since many Muslims live in very poor, deprived areas, where unemployment is high, many of them have a strong sense of social injustice and may find the fundamentalist position attractive.

There are also large numbers of Sikhs, especially in West London, who came originally from the Punjab in India, and Hindus, as well as a small but growing number of Buddhists.

Religion and schools

All state schools have to provide religious education, which must include Christianity and the other main religions found in the UK (see page 173).

There are some state schools with a specific religious focus. Church of England and Roman Catholic schools have existed for a long time and make up the majority of single-faith schools. There are also a number of Methodist and Jewish schools, and more recently some Muslim, Sikh, Greek Orthodox and Seventh Day Adventist schools have been established. The present government is keen to encourage the growth of this type of school, because some research has suggested that they may achieve better academic results than other schools. However, this is controversial and some people have expressed concerns that single-faith schools may increase the isolation and segregation of some immigrant communities. The country became much more aware of these issues during the race riots in the north of England in the summer of 2001.

The environment

Many people in England are concerned about environmental problems like reducing pollution, protecting the countryside and preserving our historical heritage. Membership of organizations concerned with these issues has grown enormously in recent years. The biggest organization is the National Trust, which was set up in 1895 by three Victorian philanthropists who were concerned about the effects of uncontrolled development and industrialization, and wanted to preserve places of historic interest or natural beauty for everyone to enjoy. Other organizations include the Royal Society for the Protection of Birds (RSPB), the Civic Trust, the Ramblers' Association, the Woodland Trust, Friends of the Earth, and the Council for the Protection of Rural England (CPRE).

The government, too, is committed to sustainable development and has introduced a number of strategies to encourage this, such as building homes on land which has been used before; this is known as a brownfield site, in contrast to a greenfield site (land which has never been built on). In the rest of this section we look in more detail at the environment in England, and find out what voluntary organizations and the government are doing to try to improve it.

Conservation and the countryside

A government agency, English Nature, is responsible for designating and maintaining Sites of Special Scientific Interest. These are the most important areas for wildlife and natural features. English Nature also supports research on nature conservation, and projects such as the species recovery programme which aims to re-introduce plants, insects and animals which have become extinct (or nearly extinct) in England. For example, the Large Blue butterfly, which had not been seen in England since 1979, has been successfully re-introduced from Sweden and is now flourishing in several areas.

In addition to its work with historic buildings (see below), the National Trust looks after several hundred miles of coastline, and 248,000 hectares of countryside on behalf of the nation.

Fox hunting

Hunting is a topic that arouses strong feelings, and in the past few years there have been heated arguments between those who want to ban fox hunting, on the grounds that it is cruel, and those who believe that as a traditional English sport it should be allowed to continue. Supporters also argue that if the fox population is not kept down by hunting, foxes will become an even greater pest to farmers than they already are. However, the majority of MPs are opposed to fox hunting, and believe that more humane methods should be used to control the numbers of foxes. They are currently discussing a proposal to make it illegal which is likely to become law within the next year or so.

Historic buildings and monuments

English Heritage is an organization dedicated to increasing the public's understanding of the past and conserving the historic environment. It is responsible for the 'listed buildings' scheme. Buildings of particular historical or architectural interest are given special status, and protected by strict rules that stop them being altered or modernized without permission. English Heritage is also responsible for what is called 'rescue archaeology' – the excavation of historical sites that are about to be built on. It often happens that when new development takes place in an old city, the initial work uncovers an ancient building – a Roman villa, perhaps, or a medieval cemetery – and there is then a race against time to excavate the site before the new building destroys it.

The National Trust takes care of around two hundred historic buildings and gardens, most of which are open to the public. It now has a membership of 2.7 million people, including many who work as volunteers at the Trust's properties.

Controlling pollution

Increasing quantities of greenhouse gases caused by human activity are leading to a rise in global temperatures, and England is no exception. Several of the hottest years since records began in 1772 were in the 1990s. The main greenhouse gas is carbon dioxide, and the two principal sources in England are power stations, on the one hand, and cars and lorries on the other. In the past thirty years, emissions of carbon dioxide from road transport have nearly doubled because of the huge increase in the overall number of vehicles on the road, even though efforts have been made to design engines that are less polluting, and to encourage people to buy smaller cars by reducing the tax on them. Emissions from power stations, on the other hand, have been reduced. This is largely because of the increase in the use of gas and nuclear energy instead of coal.

Renewable energy sources

However, there is growing pressure to generate more of our electricity from renewable sources such as the wind, waves and tidal currents. At the moment, only about 2 per cent of England's electricity comes from renewable energy sources, mainly from the wind and from burning farm and household waste, but this is supposed to increase to at least 10 per cent by 2010. In March 2001, the prime minister, Tony Blair, announced that the government was providing an extra £100 million to support the development of renewable energy technologies.

Although some people admire the elegant design of wind turbines, there is also resistance to them because most wind farms are located in areas of great natural beauty – which also happen to be the places that have the strongest and most consistent winds. It seems likely that in the future most wind farms will be offshore to avoid this problem. The sea also provides two other sources of renewable energy, the waves and the tides. These new technologies are still at an early stage of development, but the Department of Trade and Industry has recently provided substantial grants for research, development and testing of technology designed to use the power of waves and tidal currents.

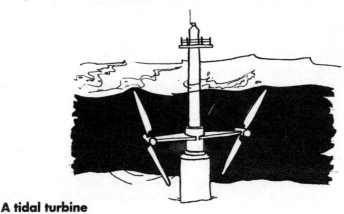

A tidal turbine

Recycling waste

Most household waste is currently put into 'landfill' sites – basically, a hole in the ground that is filled with waste and then covered over with soil. This makes no practical use of the waste, and is also potentially harmful as chemicals in the waste pollute the soil and may eventually get into the water supply. In some places the waste is burnt in special incinerators that make use of the energy produced. At present only about 8 per cent of waste is recycled, but various schemes exist to increase this. In many parts of the country there are 'bottle banks' where people can take bottles and other glass waste to be recycled. These are often accompanied by large containers for recycling newspapers, aluminium cans, and sometimes clothes and plastics.

Environmental education

To continue to protect the environment in the future, it is important for children to become aware of the environmental issues while they are still at school. Many areas of the curriculum now include topics like pollution, renewable energy, wildlife conservation and sustainable development. 'Eco Schools' is a scheme that involves teachers, pupils, parents and the local community in running their school in a way that respects and improves the environment.

GLOSSARY

Anglican relating to the Church of England

baby boom sudden increase in the birth rate

birth rate the number of babies born in a year for every thousand people

brownfield site land that has been built on before

cleric priest or minister of religion

denomination group that belongs to a particular religion, but which has slightly different views from other groups within that religion

emission the sending out of something (eg gases)

greenfield site land that has never been built on

greenhouse gas one of the gases such as methane or carbon dioxide which prevent heat escaping from the Earth's atmosphere and so cause temperatures to rise

household waste rubbish that families throw out and that is collected by the local council

labour shortage situation in which there are not enough workers to fill all the jobs available

life expectancy length of time someone is likely to live

offshore in the sea some distance from the coast

pollution making soil, water or air dirty and dangerous for living things

regenerate improve

renewable can be replaced (sun, wind, waves and tides are renewable sources of energy because they never run out; oil, coal and nuclear energy are non-renewable because they cannot be replaced)

suburbs areas away from the centre of large towns or cities where people live

sustainable development development that meets the needs of people now without compromising the needs of people in future

Taking it further

Suggested reading

Paxman, Jeremy, *The English*, Penguin, 1999
Bryson, Bill, *Notes from a Small Island*, Doubleday, 1995

A good source of detailed information about the people of England is the *UK Yearbook*, published by The Stationery Office (also see below) and updated every year.

Websites

You can download the *UK 2002 Yearbook* free from:
http://www.statistics.gov.uk

If you are interested in finding out more about the census of 1901, then go to: **http://www.pro.gov.uk**

For information about the environment and the countryside, try the following:
http://www.english-nature.org.uk
http://www.countryside.gov.uk/index.htm
http://www.defra.gov.uk/environment/index.htm

Most of the voluntary organizations concerned with the environment and conservation mentioned in this chapter have websites. Here are some of them:

http://www.nationaltrust.org.uk
http://www.english-heritage.org.uk

http://www.foe.co.uk   Friends of the Earth
http://www.rspb.org.uk
http://www.woodland-trust.org.uk

If you are interested in British government policy on renewable energy, the website below gives details:
http://www.cabinet-office.gov.uk/innovation/2001 /energy/Renewener.shtml

Details of the Eco Schools scheme can be found at:
http://www.eco-schools.org.uk

12 | ENGLAND IN THE WIDER WORLD

Imperial expansion and contraction

Britain was the predominant industrial and sea-faring nation of the nineteenth century, the leading figure in the spread of parliamentary democracy, the arts and scientific invention. At its height, the British Empire covered a quarter of the globe – an empire upon which 'the sun never sets'. In the first half of the twentieth century, the experience of two world wars and economic recession weakened it. In the second half of the twentieth century, the Empire was gradually broken up as former colonies became independent states. It was a time during which, in the famous words of the American statesman Dean Acheson, Britain had 'lost an Empire and not yet found a role'.

Constitutional reform has given regional assemblies to Scotland, Wales and Northern Ireland and may lead to further changes. The ties linking the countries which make up the UK have been loosened and questions have been raised about its future, for example should England have its own regional government? At the moment there is no public desire for one. But as constitutional changes take root, with Wales, Scotland and Northern Ireland establishing increasingly separate political identities, attitudes may change.

The Commonwealth

The Commonwealth is an organization consisting of fifty-four independent states, most of which were once part of the British Empire, and includes nearly one-third of the world's population. Established in 1931, its purpose is to promote co-operation between governments, encourage the spread of democracy and aid economic development, as well as to act as a discussion forum. It has a permanent secretariat, costing £35 million a year in 2002, to keep the organization running. Occasionally, diplomatic action is taken against governments which it is felt have acted wrongly. In 2000, Fiji was expelled when the elected government was overthrown. In 2002 Robert Mugabe's government in Zimbabwe was strongly criticized over its human rights record. The Queen is officially the head of the Commonwealth but the position is not hereditary. After she retires or dies, the head may be someone who is neither British nor a member of the Royal Family. Britain, which views itself as the first among equals of the fifty-four states, gains considerable prestige and influence from the Commonwealth. However, its importance has been in decline as the forging of links with neighbouring countries and particularly of those between Britain and the rest of Europe, have taken precedence. Countries like New Zealand and Australia felt abandoned as preferential trade agreements were given to Britain's EU partners. The future of the Commonwealth looks unclear. Any decline in its importance also has implications for the monarchy – the status of the Queen, as head of the Commonwealth, would be diminished.

Ireland

Ireland was part of the British Empire until 1926 when most of the country (subsequently called the Republic of Ireland) broke away after a bloody war of independence. Territory in the north of the country remained part of the British Empire. Today, however, relations with the Irish Republic are close and harmonious. There is a great deal of trade and movement of people between the two countries. Both governments are working together to find a solution to what is known as 'The Troubles' in the North.

'The Troubles'

The majority of Northern Ireland's population is Protestant and prefers to retain links with the UK (the unionists); the Catholic minority (about 40 per cent) would mostly favour unity with the Republic of Ireland. The violent conflicts which have characterized the North's history over the last thirty years have led to over three thousand five hundred deaths and untold misery. The violence mainly took place in the North itself but there were from time to time incidents in England. Most of the main paramilitary groups have now agreed to a cease-fire. Although there have been very occasional but serious security incidents in English cities caused by a small breakaway group from the IRA (known as the 'Real IRA'), the bombing campaign and terrorist-related incidents in England have otherwise stopped.

Attitudes towards the European Union

Although it was the Conservative Party which negotiated the UK's entry into Europe, Tony Blair's two predecessors, both Conservative prime ministers, did not enjoy good relations with the European Union. Margaret Thatcher and John Major were reluctant participants who viewed further European integration with suspicion. Tony Blair, on the other hand, said he wants to 'play a leading role in Europe'. When the EU adopted the Euro as its single currency on 1 January 2002, the UK stayed outside the 'Euro zone'. The UK government wants to wait and see what happens before making a decision about entry. Tony Blair is in favour of joining the EU's single currency providing the economic conditions are favourable (the Euro must meet 'five key economic tests') and the electorate agree in a referendum. But as everybody knows, economic data can be interpreted in various ways, especially by politicians. In the end, it will be a political, rather than an economic, decision that determines whether or not Britain adopts the Euro. In England many people, especially the Tory party, see the loss of the pound as a further step towards the loss of sovereignty, meaning that Britain will no longer be able to control its own affairs. Yet, it is hard to see the UK staying outside the Euro zone for long. The pressure from business interests to join will be strong.

Ordinary people have mixed attitudes towards the European Union – they feel it is important, but often appear to be unenthusiastic or uninterested. In the 1999 elections, the Conservatives became the largest British party in the European Parliament, but only 23 per cent of the total electorate bothered to vote. On the other hand, polls show that those who expect the European Parliament and Union to have most power over their lives in twenty years' time is twice as great as those who expect the Westminster Parliament to have most power. People expect the EU to become dominant in their lives but do not identify very strongly with Europe.

The 'special relationship' with the United States

British governments since 1945 like to talk about the 'special relationship' with the United States, based on a common language, shared notions about the value of the democratic style of government and free trade, as well as historical and cultural links. Critics say this is just nostalgia and wishful thinking on Britain's part. Undoubtedly, the relationship is more important to Britain, the less powerful partner, than to the United States which finds Britain useful mainly because of its role as a leader in Europe.

Foreign policy – the ethical dimension

Today Britain is still a significant player in world politics – one of only five permanent members of the UN Security Council and a nuclear power. Tony Blair believes it can play 'a pivotal part in the world' – hence Britain's military involvement in conflicts in Kosovo, the Gulf and Afghanistan.

On coming to power after the 1997 general election, the new Labour government declared that it also wanted to be 'a force for good in the world' and spoke of 'the ethical dimension' to foreign policy. A brave and ambitious promise. Critics have pointed to the government's dealings with dictatorships. The choice for the government can be especially difficult when they have to decide between jobs at home and, for example, allowing exports to a regime with a poor human rights record.

A centre of finance and business

Financial services make a very important contribution to the economy. London is the largest international financial centre in

Europe, and with New York and Tokyo, one of the three biggest in the world. It has more overseas banks than any other financial centre. It has the world's largest foreign exchange market, trading the largest range of currencies and is the biggest market in the world for trading foreign equities (nearly half of the global turnover in 2000). A number of factors will promote London's continued pre-eminence as a financial centre: the globalization of financial markets, the importance of English as the language of business and the development of the single market in Europe. In order to retain that importance, the financial services industries are very much in favour of joining the Euro currency.

English – a global language

The spread of English across the globe seems unstoppable. Approximately 350 million people speak it as their first language and 300 million as their second. According to *The Economist* magazine, a billion people are learning it, about a third of the world's population are in some sense exposed to it and by 2050, it is predicted, half the world will be more or less proficient in it. It is the language of globalization – of international business, politics and diplomacy. It is the language of the Internet. You'll see it on posters in Cote d'Ivoire, you'll hear it in pop songs in Tokyo, you'll read it in official documents in Phnom Penh... It is now the global language.

The future?

Here are some of the issues which are likely to dominate in the near future:

- **The relationship with Europe**: How will this develop? What impact will it have on party politics, especially the Conservative Party currently fighting its own internal battles over attitudes to Europe.
- **What does it mean to be English?** Fifty years ago, people were in less doubt about this than they are today. England is now a multicultural and multi-faith society. Scotland, Wales and Northern Ireland have devolved governments. Legal authority

for many matters rests in the European Union offices in Brussels, not in the Parliament in London. We know what England was, but we are not sure what kind of a society it is becoming.

■ **Public services (Health, Education and Transport)**: These desperately need to be improved. They form the key issues for the Labour government. It will require a lot of money and this investment will take a long time to bring about improved performance. To raise the finance needed means raising taxes which will be unpopular. Will the electorate's patience run out before the improvements begin to appear?

■ **Immigration and multiculturalism**: In recent years there have been race riots in a few English cities. There is also much controversy in the media on how to manage asylum seekers. Will the government be able to deal with these tensions and issues successfully?

We hope you have enjoyed *Teach Yourself English Language, Life & Culture* and that you will be encouraged to continue finding out about this fascinating society by investigating the websites and book references, or even come on a visit to England!

GLOSSARY

asylum seekers refugees escaping from political persecution in their own country and asking for protection in another country

cease-fire end of fighting between armies

colonies country or area which is controlled politically by a more powerful country

multi-faith many different religions

nostalgia affectionate feeling about past events

pivotal central

sea-faring connected with the sea

secretariat office responsible for managing an organization

Taking it further

For the government's ideas about what will be happening in the future: **http://www.Foresight.gov.uk**

INDEX

Other related titles